D0297617

THE LIBRARY OF PRACTICAL THEOLOGY
General Editor: Martin Thornton

TRUTHS THAT COMPELLED:
Contemporary Implications of Biblical Theology

By the same author

CONFLICT IN CHRISTOLOGY
MIRACLES AND REVELATION

TRUTHS
THAT COMPELLED

Contemporary Implications of Biblical Theology

by

STEWART LAWTON

Warden of St. Deiniol's Library

HODDER AND STOUGHTON

SBN 340 02982X I

PRINTED IN GREAT BRITAIN FOR HODDER
AND STOUGHTON LIMITED, ST. PAUL'S HOUSE,
WARWICK LANE, LONDON, E.C.4 BY C. TINLING
AND CO. LIMITED, LIVERPOOL, LONDON AND
PRESCOT

To my daughter
Wendy

EDITORIAL PREFACE

During recent years there has been a remarkable revival of interest in theological studies, covering a wide range of thought and extending to an expanding public. Whatever its underlying causes, this movement has certainly been stimulated by some bold and radical speculation, as well as by a continuing quest for greater personal responsibility in theological decision.

Those responsible for *The Library of Practical Theology* welcome these trends, while recognising that they create new problems and make new demands. Our aim is to try to be of some service in meeting this new situation in a practical way, neither taking sides in current controversy nor forcing any particular viewpoint upon our readers. We hope rather, to assist them to follow their own theological reasoning, and to interpret their own religious experience, with greater clarity. This implies a practical evaluation both of current scholarship and more popular religious thought, which in turn presupposes a certain amount of background historical theology. "A modern re-statement of traditional doctrine" necessitates a sympathetic understanding of what is being re-stated. "Contemporary trends" are hardly intelligible without some study of the historical process from which they have evolved.

A new theological interest having been awakened, we feel that the time is ripe to launch a series of this kind, and we hope that it proves not entirely false to all the implications of its title. We hope that it will develop into a true *Library*, a carefully planned corpus of practical studies and not just an interesting collection of books. By *Practical* we mean that which impinges on human experience and makes sense of the present situation. And, while avoiding the heavily technical, the Library will be unashamedly concerned with *Theology*. Our faith is that theology still holds the key to the ultimate meaning of the universe, and as the indispensable interpreter of religious experience, it is still the mainspring of the deepest human fulfilment.

MARTIN THORNTON

CONTENTS

CHAPTER ONE

Interpreting the Bible

What is biblical theology? The contexts in which the expression is used often suggest that it is something new,
all-embracing and constructive: and properly defined,
this is perfectly true. Although the ground was being long
prepared by the historical study of the Bible, biblical
theology has only become a fully conscious way of thinking
within the past half century. There is no Christian belief
or practice that has not been, or will not be, affected by it.
Whilst the study of church history reveals the imperfect
vision of succeeding ages, the Bible provides the foundation
upon which Christian thinking and action must be based.
However, just as the term *existentialist* covers the Christian
philosopher Kierkegaard, the atheist playwright Sartre
and even left-bank beatniks, so biblical theology covers
work as diverse as that of the conservative F. F. Bruce and
the radical R. Bultmann. What these men have in common
is the profound desire to understand the Bible on the
Bible's own terms. This must seem a platitude to anyone
unacquainted with the history of Christian thought, so
in order to understand the principles of interpretation
that are viable today, we must retell a little of the background story. We are now past the first flush of enthusiasm
for biblical theology, and some of the emerging problems
will also have to be discussed.

We must begin by looking at the way in which the Bible was put together and see how the beliefs about it developed. The Old Testament was the product of a very prolonged literary tradition; and the way in which it is arranged in Christian Bibles which derive from the Greek Septuagint version obscures the way it was formed and the relative importance of the books. The heart of it is the Law, Torah—Genesis to Deuteronomy—which enshrines all that the Hebrew-Jewish people believed about their divine calling and destiny. It contains the story of the people of God down to the entry into the promised land, together with their ritual and moral legislation. Israel's story was the story of God's salvation; Israel's laws were God's laws; and it was a natural step to the belief that the Pentateuch was divinely inspired. Nevertheless, the text of these documents was not treated as sacrosanct during the formative period. Modern scholarship is still engaged in unravelling the fascinating development of the Pentateuch. As late as about 300 B.C., when the Samaritan schism took place, the Bible which they took with them was the Pentateuch and nothing more.

The second great section of the Jewish Bible to be added was the Prophets. This never attained quite the same eminence as the Law, but became closely allied to it. It had three parts: the Former Prophets—Joshua, Judges, Samuel and Kings—and the Latter Prophets which consisted of (a) Isaiah, Jeremiah and Ezekiel, and (b) the Book of the Twelve (minor) prophets. The Former Prophets—the historical books—are a wonderful blending of court and temple annals with folk literature, all tightly controlled by the theology of the Law. The story of the people of God is carried forward into living experience of God as judge and redeemer. The books of the prophets are anthologies of their utterances, believed *ex hypothesi* to be inspired. These men did not create Israel's basic beliefs, as it was the tendency a generation ago to think, but they undoubtedly supplemented the tradition and deepened the understanding of its implications. Every national crisis and every aspect of man's mind and actions has a moral and therefore religious coefficient. The Prophets, like the historical books, are value-judgements passed upon history in the light of the covenant.

The third section of the Old Testament was simply called the Writings, and even in Our Lord's time its contents were not finally scheduled. Its ultimate boundaries were fixed at the rabbinic Council of Jamnia at the beginning of the second century A.D. which also produced the official Massoretic text of the Old Testament. The Greek version, made by Jewish scholars at Alexandria, contained a number of books and fragments which were never incorporated into the authorised Hebrew Bible, and these became known as the Apocrypha. The Writings in the Hebrew Bible include the books of Ruth, Esther, Lamentations, Job, Proverbs, Ecclesiastes and the Song of Solomon. This section also includes Daniel—which is now known to have been written in the second century B.C.—and the large work which we know as Chronicles, Ezra and Nehemiah. The most important item in the Writings is the Book of Psalms—the Jewish hymn-book. Just as *Hymns Ancient and Modern* contains a great range of material, from fine hymns like the *Veni Creator* to things such as Mrs. Alexander's "Within the churchyard side by side are many long low graves", so the Book of Psalms crosses the gamut of human feelings, and gives a wonderful insight in depth into Israel's public and private life of devotion.

This brings us to the next stage in biblical development. After the fall of Jerusalem in 587 B.C. the Jews no longer possessed political self-determination. Even after the return from exile they existed simply as a religious enclave within the Persian, and later the Ptolemaic, empire. Their religion became their *raison d'être*. They became the people of the *book*: the book was God's law, and to that law every detail of life must be conformed. From this arose the idea of a *canon*, a schedule of sacred books that could never be added to nor subtracted from. From this in turn grew the belief that the books were divinely inspired in the sense that they were inerrant in every detail. Both these developments, however necessary they were for the survival of Judaism, were artificial. One has only to ask what is more inspired about Esther than Ecclesiasticus to see the first point; whilst the necessity of textual criticism to all biblical study shows that we simply do not possess an exactly given test like the standard metre in the Louvre.

Judaism even in its most cloistered periods was not hermetically sealed off from surrounding culture. The older strands of Scripture show clear signs of Egyptian, Mesopotamian and Canaanite influences, as the later strands do of Greek ideas. The Jews had to live in the world in contact with Gentiles. This was especially felt at Alexandria, where even the Old Testament itself was translated into Greek. Philo, contemporary of our Lord, was a formidable scholar and philosopher by the standards of any age. He attempted to expound Judaism as a body of consistent beliefs that would stand up to comparison even with Plato. But there were banal and unedifying elements in Scripture that he found himself unable to work into his system as they stood. Greek philosophers had come up against the same problem with Homer. The all-too-human stories about the gods were out of place in the later philosophico-mystical treatises, so they had to be treated as allegories. Philo did just the same with the Old Testament. The family episodes of the patriarchs, the wars of Joshua, the tragedies of David's little court were perfectly at home in the Hebrew folk literature—and they make the Old Testament come alive to us—but they were out of keeping with a rarefied mind like Philo's. Yet Judaism had already put the seal of divine infallibility upon the canon of Scripture. There was nothing for it but to seek for allegorical interpretations: and if this method could be applied to Jacob and Esau, it could also reinterpret the Ten Commandments and the ritual code.

Orthodox rabbinic Judaism was not interested, like Philo, in trying to dress up its religion for the outside world, but it had its own problems. The religious and social practices of the Hebrews underwent considerable changes with the passing centuries; yet every detail of the tradition must now be made to seem to conform to the new image of Jewish orthodoxy. The rabbis therefore developed their own allegorical methods of interpretation. This was the inevitable consequence of their doctrine of verbal inspiration. It shows up the weakness of that doctrine more surely than any findings of higher criticism. One unhistorical approach to Scripture thus led straight to another.

Our Lord's disciples were, as far as we can see, orthodox Jews. John the Baptist's father was a temple priest, and Jesus and his followers worshipped regularly in temple and synagogue. Our Lord's every word and action echo the thought and aspirations of the Old Testament. This is not the same as saying that someone's speeches are full of quotations from Shakespeare. The Hebrew and Jewish people, and hence their scriptures, are like a living organism—not simply conditioned and programmed by the past, but always drawing towards the future. Our Lord gathers into himself the threads of aspiration in the Old Testament and by his every word and deed proclaims that they are about to be consummated. The Christian case from the very beginning was therefore partly based upon the claim that Jesus fulfilled the Old Testament. Some of the particular fulfilments seem at first sight a little artificial, but the major word-pictures which describe the person and achievement of Christ are all from the very heart of the Old Testament.

Behind the great variety of writings in the Old Testamant is a unity, expressed in a body of beliefs about the past and aspirations for the future. Modern scholarship has now highlighted this fact, so that we can speak of the theology of the Old Testament. This theology is made up of the amazing story of the people of Israel together with the religious evaluations of it. It is this combination of history and faith that made Israel unique and significant, and it is this which made it important for the men of the New Testament and for us. In the New Testament, the history and beliefs of Israel are completely taken over and transmuted.

The call of Israel, the Exodus and the covenant are lived through again—often the very same words and names are used. Peter, James and John see in a vision Moses and Elijah talking with Jesus about the exodus he is to bring about. Jericho is the first milestone to Christ's victorious passion, as it was to the first Jesus-Joshua's victorious entry into the promised land. But these things are no more than the illuminated border round the documents that enshrine the profound unity and continuity of God's re-creating work through his selected representatives.

The actual books of the New Testament, like those of the Old, came into being in different ways; and again like those of the Old Testament, beneath their diversity they share a common faith—this time, a proclamation kerygma, about what God has done for mankind in Christ. These little books were all written for groups of men and women who worshipped Jesus as their Lord—who believed that by his sufferings and victory a new chapter had been opened for mankind. They believed that fellowship in him brought reconciliation with God and the remaking of human nature in a society where all human divisions could be broken through. We cannot begin to understand the New Testament unless we realise that it was written by and to people who shared a common knowledge and adventure of faith.

That the truths of the gospel were first woven on the loom of Old Testament ideas was at first not even a practical hindrance, but rather an aid to its communication, for most of the believers in the early decades were either Jews or Gentile fellow-travellers. But with the national rejection of the new faith by the Jews, the Church was obliged to concentrate almost its whole appeal to the Graeco-Roman world. What could a concept like Messiah or even Christos mean to Greeks or Italians? The kerygma, the heart of the proclamation, was indelibly written into the apostolic writings, but it had to be taught in the thought-forms of the outside world. Apologetics is an activity in which the Church has got to engage at every epoch; and the fact has to be faced that at any particular time the Church never escapes some contamination with the spirit of the age. Professor Torrance made a

B

minute study of the Apostolic Fathers—the next group of Christian writings to come after the New Testament— and it is sad to see how the sharp edge of the gospel has already been blunted at certain points. But let any critic take one or two key concepts from the New Testament and try his hand at explaining them to someone in our day who has had a purely secular education. Today Christian intellectual effort seems bent upon two mutually contradictory pursuits. On the one hand there is the search for the *secular* meaning of the gospel. Some writers take this to mean finding out what contribution the Christian should make to the present world order; others take it to mean turning the faith itself into statements about human relationships. Then on the other hand, some of the enthusiasts for biblical theology will have nothing but biblical categories, and see nothing good in the hellenistic world, let alone in the scientific and sociological insights of the modern world. The church has got to live and work in the world, and function through the social and intellectual structures that it finds there. It is also committed to seeing the world through the eyes of the Bible (and not vice versa). Other generations produced philosophies that were biblical and secular, loyal to faith and to reason: is our generation too feeble to make the attempt?

By careful selection, it is quite easy to write of the early Christian centuries as a story of disintegration. Under God, however, it was a period of great consolidation. Powerful forces were at work which guaranteed the integrity of the kerygma. One of these was Christian worship, centred as it was upon word and sacrament. Baptism and the eucharist, together with the gradually emerging Christian year and daily offices inspired by belief in the presence of the victorious Lord, made the faith live in every active Christian mind. Much has been learned about the cohesive power of worship in all civilisations: the Church's understanding of itself greatly magnified the natural sociological effects of its worship. Another consolidating force was the formation of the Church's creeds and definitions. The series of heresies which reached their zenith in the fourth and fifth centuries obliged the church to formulate its faith especially in regard to the Trinity and the Incarnation. The heresies themselves and the orthodox counter-structure seem far removed from the language of the New Testament—let alone the problems for religion in our own day—but there can be no doubt that the adoption of any one of the heresies as the established faith would have cut the heart out of the kerygma. Gibbon could sneer at Christendom being split over a diphthong, but that diphthong meant the difference between believing that Christ is a demi-god—something like God—or believing that God himself is personally disclosed in him.

It is in the light of this work of consolidation in liturgy and creed that we should see the fixing of the canon, the schedule of sacred books. The Old Testament was accepted *en bloc*, and with it the rabbinic doctrine of its inerrancy. This did not go unchallenged. Marcion, who founded an influential break-away sect in the second century, would have none of it. He believed that some of the religious ideas of the Old Testament were incompatible with the gospel, and he refused to accept allegorical interpretation as a subterfuge. Marcion has many sympathisers today who feel like the little girl who, after being told that the God of the New Testament is the same as the God of the Old, replied "Oh, hasn't he improved!"

To the Old Testament were added the apostolic writings that we call the New Testament. It would seem strange to

most Christians today that there was a time when responsible leaders had reservations about the inclusion of St.
John's Gospel or the Epistle to the Hebrews, but the
Church had to thrash out the relative value of its credentials and the process took centuries to complete. We sometimes still hear the phrase "It was the New Testament
which created the Church." Historically speaking this is
nonsense. The books of the New Testament were selected
(a) because they were thought to be genuine writings of
the apostles or their companions and (b) because they embodied the Church's faith. It is therefore unscholarly to try
to study the New Testament in isolation from the tradition
of the Church which published it. This does not mean that
the Church possesses a set of extra beliefs that have been
handed down separately from Scripture, which can be
brought out of the hat to prove this or that doctrine. What
it does mean is that the New Testament cannot be used in
evidence against the Church, and made to say things in
contradiction to what we know of the Early Church's faith
from its liturgy, creeds, and theological treatises. The
New Testament writers do not claim for themselves any
special divine authority except when they are quoting our
Lord's explicit words and commands—and even here the
writers of the gospels take great liberties with each other's
scripts. This is a fact, however shocking it may sound to
some ears. Belief in the inspiration of the New Testament
is an evaluation placed upon it by the believing community
of Christians.

Jewish rabbinic beliefs about the way the Old Testament
was inspired were inherited by the Church along with the
scriptures themselves, and it was not easy for scholars to
take an independent line. The fulfilment of Old Testament
prophecy was a major factor in Christian apologetics, and

this inevitably brought with it the allegorical interpretation of Scripture. To say that Christ fulfils the rôle of the
Suffering Servant is not the same thing as saying that
Isaiah 52.13–53.12 is an allegory about Christ; but in
patristic times there seemed no practical alternative to
rabbinic fundamentalism and its corollaries.

Christian allegorisation was developed systematically
at Alexandria, the very city where Philo had worked. It
had precedent in the New Testament—in the argumentation of the Epistle to the Hebrews and the Moses typology
of the gospels. Clement opened up the method in the
second century and Origen offered a thoeretical justification for it in the fourth book of his *Peri Archon*. His commen-
taries on Scripture and other treatises provided the first
weighty systematic theology to appear. We know that
educated pagans such as Celsus and Porphyry sneered at
the banality of the Old Testament, and it is obvious that
the early theologians were embarrassed by the Jewish
scriptures. The search for the *inner* meaning of Scripture
thus had a strong apologetic motive—Bultmann in his
search for a demythologised gospel has even been compared to Origen. Every passage of Scripture, Origen
believed, had a series of meanings—of which the literal
meaning is often of quite subsidiary importance. It
should be remembered that by *literal* he often means the
naïve sense. No one would imagine that "the arm of the
Lord" was meant to be taken in the literal sense. The
Bible is full of analogical language like this: the question—
and it is a live issue today—is where we are to draw the
line. How true is any of the biblical language that ascribes
personal activity to God? The vast majority of Christians
today would agree with Origen's comments on some passages, as when he says that the six days of creation are not

to be taken literally. The Alexandrians often sound modern and commonsense; but their method went much further. They tried to find mystical and dogmatic truths wrapped up in all manner of Old Testament stories. Some of us are still so familiar with sermons spun round texts like "ivory, apes and peacocks" that we do not at first realise how odd the allegorical method can become. There is a significant modicum of justification in the New Testament for reading back doctrinal truths into the Old. The rock which "followed" the Israelites in the wilderness is said by St. Paul to have been Christ (1 Cor.10.4). Here once again is a question that has come to the fore in our own day. A profound interest has arisen in biblical typology. Not only are symbolic words and evocative word-pictures continually being combined and contrasted, but historical situations like the Exodus are alluded to or relived. This is analogous to the way in which poetry uses language and imagery to convey a complexity of meaning in depth. It is quite another matter to make the clock go round backwards, and literally to discover the New Testament in the Old.

It was inevitable that the inspiration of the New Testament should come to be thought of in the same way as that of the Old. This added a fresh range of problems for the exegetes. There was the question of how the four gospels were to be harmonised with one another. There were passages where a literal interpretation would be unconvincing—surely, said Origen, we do not imagine that Jesus saw all the kingdoms of the world from a single mountain! But there was more at stake than devotional interest, as confrontation with the heresies was to demonstrate. In the second century, gnostic teachers were claiming to possess a secret tradition for interpreting the

Scriptures supposed to have been handed down from the apostles to the spiritual élite. Why were they so anxious to have Christianity with a difference? St. Paul tells us that the Cross is foolishness to the Greeks—and indeed the whole idea of the transcendent God taking manhood was unthinkable as it literally stands in the New Testament. If Jesus was divine, he ate and drank only to give the appearance of manhood. Hence the name *docetic* for this type of thinking from the Greek word to *seem* or *appear*. The Son of God could not have been crucified: either his divinity forsook his body before the Passion, or someone else such as Simon of Cyrene was crucified in his place. Such ingenuity shows how deep were the motives inhibiting men from believing that God could really involve himself in our world. Even Greek orthodoxy eventually settled on a formula which seems to suggest that Christ's sufferings were external to the being of God himself. A much more subtle form of the docetic problem was offered in the fourth century by the followers of Arius. For several critical decades this type of doctrine practically dominated Christendom. According to the Arians, Christ as Son of God was a created being, not identical with the Godhead in the last analysis.

The Christian fathers developed two main lines of constructive refutation against this whole range of deviations. On the one hand, the Alexandrian scholars marshalled every jot of New Testament evidence which pointed to our Lord's true deity. On the other hand, Antiochene theologians held that an objective study of the gospels shows Jesus Christ as truly divine and truly human. Both aspects must be given their true weight, they argued. The union of God and man in Christ they tended to speak of in psychological rather than in ontological language.

Only if a genuinely literal and historical method was used for interpreting the gospels could the two essential sides of Christ's person be grasped and safeguarded. The scholars of Antioch were sure that Origen had sold the faith down the river by admitting non-literal interpretations into the gospels—by speaking, for instance, of the marks of Christ's manhood, his eating and sleeping, as assumed for purposes of conformity to our condition. St. Luke says that Jesus grew in wisdom: we cannot begin to study his life if we do not take statements like this seriously.

The church of Antioch had a long tradition of active biblical scholarship. Its fruits can best be studied in the work of Diodore of Tarsus and that of his two famous pupils Chrysostom and Theodore of Mopsuestia. Although they shared to the full the Greek metaphysical approach to doctrine, the members of the school had a striking independence in their approach to Scripture. The Hebrew language was studied, and there were even contacts with eminent Jewish exegetes. Theodore (d. 428) denied the canonicity of the catholic epistles, including James— which not only shows his independence of scholarly judgement but reveals the fact that even in the early fifth century there was no slavish conformity to established beliefs about the canon of the New Testament. In their opposition to Origen and his allegorising, the Antiochenes were led to argue that the Prophets actually foresaw the coming of Christ. This, needless to say, was not a helpful solution. These scholars were at their best with the New Testament. It shows genuine historical acumen when they say that the disciples never confessed Jesus as divine during his lifetime, but only after Pentecost. From these controversies of the fourth and fifth centuries we can see that the method by which the Bible is to be interpreted is of no mere academic concern but has a direct bearing upon the faith of every Christian.

As the patristic age merged into the middle ages, the realism of Antiochene theology was left behind, and the allegorical method became ever more deeply entrenched in Christian thinking. One has only to look at the subject-headings in the Authorised Version of the Song of Solomon to see how naturalised it had become. It was especially dear to the men of the middle ages because the whole world of nature was also a picture book to them of moral and spiritual lessons. But with the middle ages came also the founding of the universities of Western Europe, and with them the teaching of systematic theology in an academic rather than a devotional framework. The men of the Reformation and of the scientific revolution saw nothing in scholasticism but pedantry and obscurantism: yet these revolutions had their beginnings in the older system, and we can see the halting search for a more historical approach to theology centuries before Erasmus. One Victorine scholar even dared to say that Isaiah 7.14 in the Hebrew text does not support the doctrine of the virgin birth of our Lord. But the real protagonist of the new ways was St. Thomas Aquinas himself. How up to date he was can be judged from this fact. When he began his teaching career, knowledge of Aristotle was beginning to seep into the west by way of the Arabs, and the study of him was being proscribed as dangerous in one university after another. Aquinas grasped the nettle and used what he could of Aristotle to create his own theological system. Much of his work turns on the belief that our principal avenue to the truth is the analysis of created things as they are actually known. It is not surprising, then, that he calls for the literal meaning of Scripture to be the cardinal factor in its interpretation. No doctrine, moreover, ought to be based on allegorical interpretations alone. This sounds a modest request, but it was a notable advance at the time. Aquinas also maintained the right of reason to have a voice in scriptural exegesis. He would not of course have admitted a reading that was in flat contradiction to the teaching of the Church: he would not have understood the modern attempts to drive a wedge between the Bible and the community which canonised it.

Scholasticism prepared the way for the Reformation, but in regard to the Bible, the Reformation had a dream of its own. Once the Bible was set free from ecclesiastical authority and made available to the people, its light would shine out to all men unequivocally. The warring sects of the sixteenth century soon shattered this delusion. Luther set up the Bible as the supreme authority in faith and morals, but the final arbiter was the judgement of the individual believer. Some of Luther's own private judgements show a remarkable independence when compared with the standards of later Protestant orthodoxy. James he rejected as an epistle of straw: not since the fifth century had a Christian leader entered a query against a New Testament document. It was undoubtedly the fresh look at the Bible which gave the sudden revolutionary twist to the religious discontents of the age. Rediscovered biblical insights did not simply challenge accepted Church discipline and sacramental practice, they produced a permanent shift in men's picture of their relationship to God. The Reformation was, in truth, a step towards a biblical theology. In the actual way the Bible was handled, the changes must not be exaggerated. Despite the great changes in worship and church order, the men of the Reformation were much nearer to the middle ages than they are to us when it comes to exegesis. Luther's doctrine of the consubstantiation of the sacramental species with the body of Christ is a highly sophisticated scholastic reconstruction.

Protestantism soon settled into rigid orthodox patterns of its own, which remained substantially undisturbed until the coming of the liberal theologies of the nineteenth century. Calvin's Geneva experiment and the religious settlements in Britain, Germany and Scandinavia were necessary and inevitable; the Bible simply could not be allowed to exist *in vacuo*. It was only practicable as the rule of faith in the context of an accepted tradition of discipline, worship and belief.

While the efforts of Erasmus and Luther to secure a more objective study of the Bible were being lost sight of in the Protestant orthodoxies of the seventeenth century, new forces were taking shape that were destined to affect Christian thinking far more profoundly than the Reformation had done. Books are still being written about science and religion which seem to imagine that the subject can be dealt with on the periphery of Christian doctrine. Geology and Genesis, miracles and the laws of nature, biology and the fall—these are the topics on which a *modus vivendi* is sought, and with a considerable degree of success. But the scientific revolution, which got under way in the seventeenth century, affects religion at its very heart, because it profoundly altered men's image of their relationship to the universe. Anyone who takes the trouble to read Spinoza's *Tractatus Theologico-Politicus* of 1670 will find in this powerful book of three centuries ago many of the ideas that are being canvassed today as *new theology*— such as the complete demythologising of God and the supernatural and a rationalist approach to morals. From

the scientific revolution there also developed in the
eighteenth and nineteenth centuries a new way of looking
at history and ancient documents. With this the church
was forced to grapple: Christian scholars had to learn to
use every modern technique to ascertain and verify its
historical credentials. This is a story too complicated to
tell here, for the scholarly study of the Bible has been
carried out by men of every shade of heterodoxy as well
as by traditionalists. Here we are concerned to highlight
the principles which came to be regarded as inescapable
in a genuinely historical approach.

The cry of nineteenth-century scholarship was that the
Bible must be studied like any other set of ancient documents, with no holds barred. Questions about what
actually happened must not be avoided because the Bible
is sacred: if it is genuine, it will stand up to scrutiny—it
does not require dogmas or miracles to support it. Today
this point of view is accepted by all academic biblical
scholars, and over large areas it has yielded results of the
highest importance for Christian faith. There are regions,
none the less, where historical criticism has little to say.
Christian faith is not only concerned with what happened,
but with what it meant—it recognises the handwriting of
God in a historical story. Now historiography—the
technical elucidation of history—cannot by its very terms
of reference step outside the web of natural causes and
effects that make up the story of mankind. There are also
particular events recorded in the Bible about which the
historian as such can say nothing decisive. A historian
without presuppositions simply does not exist. The
evidence for our Lord's resurrection cannot be considered
in vacuo. A historian without religious beliefs will deny its
occurrence and offer natural reasons for the emergence of

the belief. A scholar imbued with Christian values, on the other hand, will be accused of introducing false elements into his studies. At the same time it should not be forgotten that as far as history in the Bible goes, a very wide agreement is possible between believing and non-believing scholars about the course of events. There is always the occasional publicity seeker who advertises ultra-sceptical views as if they represented the consensus of scholarship. The historical study of Scripture is not a passing phase, it is a permanent element in theological reflection. We cannot put the clock back to some date before this knowledge became available any more than men can pretend to forget how to explode atoms. To use reason in the study of the Bible is not a philosophical option but a sheer necessity.

To begin with, the Bible has been transmitted to us through an enormous number of hand-written copies. What we possess of the ancient manuscripts range from the great codices like Sinaiticus to tiny bits of papyrus. If one makes the experiment of copying out a few pages from a book, it will be found that one or two tiny variations from the original have crept in. The science of collating the tens of thousands of variant readings in the manuscripts of the Scriptures is called textual criticism. It is a highly skilled technical operation with its own expertise, and a remarkably high percentage of agreement between scholars is achieved.

Historical criticism—or higher criticism as it is often called to distinguish it from textual criticism—tries to do two things with a document. It seeks to find out what actually happened in history, and it attempts to discover what was in the writer's mind, what were his ideas and beliefs. Form criticism is a further technique for penetrating even behind the documents. By studying the patterns in the literary material, we can often discern the kind of source, even an oral source. Among the major achievements of historical criticism applied to the Bible are the unravelling of the sources of the Pentateuch, the matching-up of the history of the Hebrews in Palestine with archaeological discoveries, the correct locating of the second part of the book of Isaiah in the sixth century B.C., the Maccabean dating of the book of Daniel, the literary relationship of the first three gospels disclosed, and above all the locating of the principal New Testament teaching about Christ right in the first century A.D. The meaning and message of biblical books has come to light as never before. We can reconstruct the story and faith of the people of God more fully than any previous Christian age. Historical criticism cannot *prove* that God was at work, what it can do is to offer a very strong prima facie case for the unique character of biblical experience.

The nineteenth-century pioneer constructors of biblical criticism have, however, been faulted for allowing their philosophical predelictions to colour their picture of salvation history. Hegelian dialectic, romanticism, belief in historic evolution and inevitable progress, have all been alleged against them. Minds of great stature like Schleier-macher, Ritschl, Wellhausen, Harnack and Herrmann, have been unwarrantedly denigrated since the second world war. The blame can hardly be laid at their door if their high principles were diluted into a liberal religion without colour or taste. There is a modicum of truth in the criticisms: if we look at Harnack's *What is Christianity?* or Herrmann's *Communion with God* we can see that despite their lofty idealism, something of the Bible's sharp edge of divine judgement and redemption has been blunted. A

few penetrating minds recognised this all along. Kierkegaard (1813–55) almost unknown outside Denmark in his
lifetime, held that liberalism was a travesty of Christianity. P. T. Forsyth wrote books before the first world
war on the same theme—which came into their own thirty
years later.

The beginning of biblical theology as a deliberate
revolt against previous systems and attitudes was sym-
bolised by the appearance in 1919 of Karl Barth's commentary on the Epistle to the Romans. The tragedy of the
first world war and its aftermath made many young
Christians, especially on the continent, only too eager to
hear Barth's clarion call. Men must hear what the Bible
says, whether it is unpleasant or disturbing or even
incredible: they must hear and obey. If they build a
theology, it must be based upon the word of God and its
thought-forms. Every philosophical or social concept
must be subject to criticism by the norms of the Bible.
God's word is God's revelation—all non-biblical philosophical systems are ultimately man-made pretentions and
fall down like packs of cards when God's word hits them.
Barth was soon followed by a galaxy of scholars; but far
more didactic than the learned books was the revelation of
satanic evil in the Nazi terror. In the providence of God,
Barth's theology came in time to inspire many men with a
faith that was stout enough to ride through the storms of
fear and doubt.

Today Barth's theological system as he conceived it has
not nearly so many scholarly adherents as it had twenty
years ago. But this detracts very little from the achievement
of the Barthians. They created a positive approach to the
Bible that can never be given up as long as Christianity is
true to itself. The Bible is revelation or it is nothing. It is

not a tale of human achievement but of what God has said and done. Brunner, the Niebuhrs, Torrance and others have shown abundantly how biblical theology can be brought to bear upon every kind of doctrinal and cultural question. Roman Catholic theology, so long isolated from the Christian world around, now begins to feel the breath of biblical theology. Roman Catholic experts have long played their part in technical fields—like Roland de Vaux, discoverer of the community site at Qumran; but now one cannot read the works of Kung, Rahner and Congar without realising that biblical theology is penetrating even the confines of dogmatics.

As time has gone on, some of the principles laid down by Barth and his immediate followers have been seen to require a great deal more clarification and modification when we come to the actual work of studying the text of the Bible. Biblical theology is therefore being subjected to intense scrutiny from within. Some of the chief points at issue are the following.

When biblical thought was seen to have a quite distinctive ethos, it was natural to attach the word *Hebrew* to it, and to contrast it—not only with the rest of the ancient near east—but with *Greek* thought in the widest sense. This was a relatively new attitude: Calvin was no liberal theologian, but he had been glad to point to agreements between the Bible and Plato. The Barthian type of theologian tried to draw sharp distinctions between everything Hebrew and everything Greek. The fathers, it was held, had well-nigh blotted out biblical thought beneath their metaphysics. Histories of particular Christian doctrines were written like Sleeping Beauty stories—showing how Prince Charming Luther rescued the Bible from a millennium and a half of slumber. Barth himself has latterly had to protest against what he calls the witch hunt for Greek ideas in Christian writings.

Yet, as we saw earlier, the Hebrews did not live in spiritual isolation. Their genius lay not only in their God-given insights but in their ability to metabolise elements from outside. Jesus had the whole wealth of the Old Testament upon which to draw for his teaching and life pattern: the men of the Old Testament had no such reservoir—they often used old international myths to express their meaning. The biblical doctrine of the future life has often been said to be radically different from the Greek—a gift of resurrection, as opposed to natural immortality. Yet the Orphic sects were far ahead of the Jews in time regarding the state of the blessed dead. The enthusiasm for everything Hebrew has to be tempered by the facts. Nor is this merely a matter of antiquarian interest—theories about man's relationship to God, like those advanced in Nygren's *Agape and Eros*, have been put forward on the basis of a supposed conflict between biblical and Greek thought.

The anti-hellenic fervour was understandable to some extent: distinctive biblical assertions now stood out like the sheer precipices of the Alps—to use Barth's own favourite language. What is more disturbing is the anti-intellectualism of some of his followers. Luther himself had played down the philosophy of religion, for faith must not be buttressed by human contrivance; and despite the massive contribution of nineteenth-century theologians to religious philosophy, the feeling against it revived in Barthianism. Intense interest in biblical studies has even attracted a disproportionate number of students to its disciplines, and left far too few men and women to cope with the frontiers of religion and philosophy. This is not
c

the place to discuss the relations of natural and revealed religion, but the *Honest to God* and the *God is dead* debates do seem to show that biblical dogmatism cannot survive without an infra-structure of sound religious philosophy. The anti-intellectualism of early Barthianism chimed in with the twentieth-century obsession with the non-rational elements in human personality. This represents no doubt a true awareness of the chaotic forces that lie just beneath man's consciousness and the surface of society. But religion ought to bring light, and order and purpose—not add to the muddle! Then again, how is revelation actually conveyed? The older orthodoxies, both Catholic and Protestant, assumed that the most important things in the Bible were propositions, precise statements about the nature of God, the destiny of man, and the means of redemption. The truth of these statements was thought to be vouched for by miracles and the fulfilment of prophecy. Now it was realised long before Barth that the Bible is not really like this. Revelation was given in the whole providential story of Israel and above all in the very person and personality of Jesus Christ. He is the word made flesh; in him is grace and truth. Some theologians, however, have gone further, and talk as though the whole essence of revelation was the *saving event*. But what if the event never happened? or did not happen as the Bible describes it? Some writers have combined their *saving event* theology with an amazing degree of historical scepticism. This is not wholly out of keeping with the Lutheran desire to keep faith autonomous from reason and factual certitude. English theologians can never remain happy with a position that does not link the creed inextricably with belief in the occurrence of the story of salvation.

The words in Scripture, moreover, play just as important a part as the events, whether they are the prophetic evaluations at the time of the event or later comment. This is recognised in practice, for the past half century has witnessed a study of biblical terminology hitherto unparalleled. The greatest monument to this task is the *Theological Wordbook of the New Testament* edited by G. Kittel. One of our first tasks should be to understand what the various writers meant by words like *kingdom, grace* and *truth*. Disastrous mistakes have been made by people who supposed that certain words were used throughout the Bible in just the same way as they were used in their own sect or school. The labour of studying Bible words has been so Herculean that one or two scholars today are pausing to point out that philology is not the sum of theology but only a handmaiden. A word is part of a sentence; and that sentence is either spoken in, or describes, a unique human situation. The technical and symbolic language of the Bible must be looked at through the meaning of the whole revelation of God, man and nature.

It is ironical that the study of biblical words should have reached its fruition at the very time when the dominant philosophical school in Britain denies the very meaningfulness of religious language. In 1936, A. J. Ayer published his *Language, Truth and Logic*. For sheer dogmatism, this book rivals Pius IX and Mao Tse Tung. Every utterance concerning God, the supernatural, the transcendent and the nature of substance and existence can be demonstrably shown to be without the slightest factual meaning, he declares. A great deal of hard work has had to be put into the validation of religious language. This is turning out to be more than a mere defence of traditional ways of thinking. New light is being shed upon the ways in which religion uses its words. Nor is there simply *one* religious language as opposed, say, to scientific language. Wittgenstein, the father of linguistic philosophy, came in his later years to realise that we play a variety of "word-games", as he put it. Origen long ago realised that the Bible does not use its words univocally, and that disastrous absurdity comes from trying to interpret Scripture in one and the same sense throughout. The Bible speaks many languages and woe betide those who do not give due weight to them all. Often several word-games are contained in the same passage, like the various allusions within a poem.

The Bible speaks the language of myth: for man cannot be saved from blind destiny by the language of the electricity generating station but only by the word of a personal God.

The Bible speaks the language of history: for here God has acted, and here we must meet him in the world of typewriters and toothbrushes.

The Bible speaks the language of law: for man must conform to nature and to society in order to have the freedom to be himself.

The Bible speaks the language of judgement: for every human act embodies a man's values, and involves its own consequences.

The Bible speaks the language of religion: for even the love of neighbour can become an idolatry without conscious attention to God in cult and prayer.

The Bible speaks the language of love: for despite appearances, this is God's ultimate will for man and his unconditioned demand upon him.

CHAPTER TWO

The Old Testament becomes news

Within the past thirty years, a deep change has come about in the perspective of Old Testament studies. It can even be compared to the revolution produced by the first coming of historical criticism, though it is much more subtle in its effects. It is so recent that its consequences for dogmatic theology have not yet been assessed—let alone its bearing on pastoral thinking. A body of closely-knit Hebrew beliefs has been highlighted, which almost certainly were the dynamic of Israel's faith. So deeply is the New Testament involved with the Old that the basic Hebrew beliefs cannot but affect the Church of Christ; and pastors should now sit down with their people to consider their implications. The Oxford Movement began with the insight of a group of scholars, but it would not have got off the ground had its ideas never been tried out in worship, discipline and social responsibility at parochial level.

The changed outlook can be put in this way. Suppose one set out to write a book about Napoleon: one might find to begin with that his views about morals, politics and economics were very close to those of any educated European at the end of the eighteenth century. Then one day the question would suddenly thrust itself forward—

if Napoleon was so like the world of his day, what was it about him that made him so amazingly different? Something similar has happened in the study of the Old Testament. When the remains of the cities of the ancient near east began to be scientifically studied in the last quarter of the nineteenth century, and the cuneiform script of Mesopotamia and the hieroglyphics of Egypt could actually be deciphered, the first thing that struck scholars was the apparent similarity between the religious practices of Israel and her neighbours. Anthropological studies also revealed parallels to Old Testament ideas from China to Peru. Could it not be shown that the religion of the Hebrews was a member of the common stock, which later generated superior ethical ideas, which in turn fitted it to survive into the hellenistic era and so to become part of the inheritance of western culture?

The history of the Hebrews came to be rewritten in such a way as to embody this thesis. In traditional Jewish and Christian thought, the complete ritual and ethical code came from the time of Moses; the task of the prophets had been to recall the people to their ancient faith and to predict the messianic age. What is often called the Graf-Wellhausen hypothesis turned all this upside down. In the stories of the patriarchs we see traces of animism and polydaemonism. Moses introduced the fugitive Hebrews to the storm-god Jahveh, round whom a national cult developed. Contact with Canaanite civilisation widened the Israelites' horizons and also caused a creative tension between their nomadic ideals and urban life. The prophets from Amos to Deutero-Isaiah transformed the cult into an ethical monotheism which denied the existence of other gods. The Law was progressively written up to embody the new theological and ethical beliefs.

But as with our imaginary student of Napoleon, a moment of truth has arrived for Old Testament studies. What did make the religion of Israel such a radical point of departure in the ancient world?

First, there has been a great increase during the twentieth century in our knowledge about the ancient near east. The patriarchs did not live at the dawn of human consciousness—there are the remains of a settled community at Jericho five thousand years before the time of Abraham. The Sumerian civilisation of the fourth millennium B.C. had a sophisticated theology, a pantheon with a supreme being, Enlil, and a hierarchy of subordinate supernatural beings. In the mid-fourteenth century B.C. Egypt might have officially accepted a monotheistic religion but for the vested interest of the priests. Of even closer interest for Old Testament study is the world of Canaanite beliefs opened up by the discovery of the Ras-shamra tablets. This remarkable member of the ancient near eastern family also has its developed pantheon, presided over by El and his consort. If Abraham and his family had held some of the views ascribed to them by earlier biblical critics, they would indeed have been backwoodsmen by the standards of their own times. To suggest today that any belief in the Old Testament was not held until the eighth century B.C. is to build upon the sand.

But secondly, the most important factor making for reassessment has come from the closer study of Scripture itself. The critical study began with the disentangling of the documents that make up the Pentateuch, and this set the pattern. The main interest came to be centred upon the *differences* between the sources, and the *differences* between the prophets and the law. There are real dif-

ferences, and they are important for understanding how
the word of God was heard in different ages and under
different circumstances; but to put the differences at the
forefront was to miss the wood for the trees with a ven-
geance. The most important fact about a person is the
continuity of his personal identity—not the changing of
his molecules or his clothes. The unity of the Old Testament, the persistence of its characteristic basic beliefs
through the centuries of national weal and woe—this is
the astounding fact. To apprehend the bonds that unite
such different books as Genesis and the Psalms is to see
that there is such a thing as the *theology of the Old Testament*, and major books are now written with these words
as their title—a notion that would have seemed eccentric
before the second world war. Long-neglected doctrines
have come to life again: and it is precisely some of these
that are of practical importance for Christians today. In
New Testament studies, nineteenth-century liberal theologians tried to cut out of the Gospels the specifically
Jewish elements in favour of universal ethical principles;
and Schweitzer blew up the edifice by showing that the
discarded doctrines were at the heart of Jesus' message.
So with the Old Testament, it is precisely Israel's beliefs
about her own call and destiny that are the key to her
history and religion. The story begins with the certainty of
a personal call from God: the unfinished story ends with
the vision of a unique role in the remaking of mankind.

The older hypothesis that Hebrew religion gradually
improved in its ethical content, even if it were completely
demonstrable, misses the cardinal point. The heart of
Hebrew religion is not ethical principles but faith in the
one true God who calls his people, and continually redeems
those whom he has called to know him. The prophets

would certainly have denied that there was any im-
provement at all in Israel's morals as time went on. What
they affirm is the steadfastness of God's character, his
judgement and his saving love. When the basic Hebrew
beliefs are taken together, they do indeed turn out to be a
new creation. If we must have an analogy from biology,
let us call it a mutation. Even this is quite inadequate:
the Manx cat is a mutation, and it is not even aesthetically
satisfactory. Just as we denigrate the Renaissance by
talking about it as if it were only a rehash of classical
culture, so the grandeur of the Old Testament must be
looked at as a unique fact in history and not fitted into
some general cultural movement of the old world.

Many readers of this book will have received their
theological teaching in the milieu of the pre-war era, and
will now be legitimately asking what has become of the
Graf-Wellhausen hypothesis? Is the clock being turned
right back, and the Law put back before the prophets
both in time and in credal priority? The answer at the
present day, put very briefly, is as follows.

The prophets did play a creative role, but the seminal
truths of Israel's unique faith were there already, waiting
to be developed. The belief in Israel's divine call had been
the very pin that held the tribes together for centuries
before the canonical prophets. The Law also did develop,
from source J to the priestly code. But source J is not a
mumbo-jumbo of primitive superstitions—it is a clearly
thought-out account of the story of salvation. If one had to
single out a particular achievement of Biblical theology in
the Old Testament field, it might well be the reappraisal of
the early Pentateuchal sources. Generations of students
were made to learn about J E, D and P, but few, even of the
experts, got down to enquiring why these documents ever

came to be written. If, however, we begin with the Bible's own assumption that the Israelites were held together by their belief in a divine call, sealed by the Exodus and Covenant at Sinai, J and E come to life. They are the earliest known stories of God's salvation, written not just as foundation deeds for the nation but for recital at the national festivals, where God's mercies and demands were heard, and loyalty was once again pledged. The story of the Hebrews is richer and more complex than was envisaged either by the old fundamentalism or by the early exponents of historical criticism. The documents unfold an ever-continuing drama, in which God's word is continually being proclaimed, and loyalty and martyrdom mingle with blatant apostasy.

Settled on the great land route between Egypt and Mesopotamia, to say nothing of Canaanite influences on their very doorstep, the Hebrews lived in no pious ghetto: the abiding wonder is that their tradition survived one century after the settlement. Even the rigorous attempt to preserve a pure-blood Judaism was a post-exilic ideal: King David had a Moabite great-grandmother. Israel's cultic debt to other nations was especially great. The strength of their religion was its power to sort out the ideas and customs from outside, to demythologise and adapt what could be made into part of the tradition. After the conquests of Alexander the Great in 336–323 B.C. the same thing became true of Jewish proximity to the Greek world. This needs to be pointed out, as was shown in the previous chapter, in view of the over-enthusiasm in the last half-century for everything distinctively Hebrew. In the same way, some scholars have been tempted to take a single thread from the Old Testament and weave it into a thesis that this is the whole or essence of Hebrew religion.

For example, it has been said that the belief that God acted in history is the distinctive creed of Israel—but Chemosh, the Moabite god, is also said by his devotees to act in history like Jahveh.

Nevertheless, when we take the Old Testament as a whole out of the complex of Hebrew religion and Judaism after it, there comes a religion with a unique personality. That uniqueness cannot be pinned down either to the characteristics of the Hebrew language nor to one specific mode of revelation. For when we come down to bedrock, what matters most for Christians is not only what they believed, but the Old Testament men themselves. These men with their history and faith are *our* fathers. The Old Testament was on the way to becoming a well-nigh useless book for Christians, because all the interest was being centred upon its beliefs and how they evolved. But the men of the Old Testament were our forefathers in faith: what happened to them in their relations with God matters to us. They are not prehistoric curiosities: the basic conditions of man's life *vis-à-vis* God and his neighbour have not changed. The one difference for us is not our external civilisation but the coming of Christ. We shall later see the difference this makes: for the moment, the important thing is to recognise the continuity. The New Testament speaks about a "new man" even a "new heaven and earth", but never about a "new Israel". The simple reason is that the men of the New Testament never dreamed that they were a *new* Israel— they *were* Israel. They were one with God's people from Abraham: every word and deed of Christ presupposes this. St. Paul speaks of "our father Abraham"; and in 1 Corinthians 10, recalling the temptations of the Israelites in the desert, he says "our fathers" went through the sea. The comparison between the Hebrews on their trek and the newly won Christians at Corinth is especially poignant: in both cases, men who should have been filled with joy and gratitude were falling headlong into unbelief. Then, almost in an aside, St. Paul says that the rock from which the Israelites drank was Christ—and he meant it. The work of God, revealing and redeeming, is a single continuous act of his own self-giving love. The climax is reached when Jesus is born and dies and rises again, and the Spirit fills the Church; but God's character and intentions are the same all the way through.

This does not mean that we can read the whole of the New Testament into the Old. Some enthusiasts have tried to do this, and have argued that the person and work of Christ should be our primary guide to the interpretation of every Old Testament passage. But this can only be attempted by plunging into a maze of, quite frankly, unconvincing allegorisations. The doctrines of God's call and covenant, of his grace, law and judgement, above all, Israel's unquenchable faith in the future: all these are doubly valid when seen in the light of Christ's achievement. The New Testament is full of typological comparisons and contrasts with the Old. This is not make-believe, it shows God's dealings with his people as a continuous story of promise and fulfilment. The Old Testament is very helpful in this respect, that it pictures God's future acts as an enlarged repetition of the past. This is not like the Greek cyclic view of history: it is God's keeping faith, performing acts of love which are a first instalment of far greater wonders to come. There is to be a new covenant, a new heaven and earth and a new Eden, a new happy time like Israel's first days of faithfulness.

The difference between the Testaments can perhaps be

described like this, when we speak of the history of specific beliefs. The former revelation came into a world where only natural religion existed. Genesis 1–11 gives a vivid picture of the ever-increasing chaos and plight of man. When we compare these chapters with the folklore of any other people in the ancient world, we can see how drastically demythologised they are. However we picture to ourselves the origins of evil, we have to live with the fact of the loss of innocence, the grip of evil, alongside our wistful belief in the better self. With Genesis 12, the call of Abraham, new things begin to happen. Fresh truths about God and man come to light: but in the happenings of the people of God, beliefs and actions belonging to the sphere of natural religion still peep through. All the way down Israel's history there is a tug-of-war between revealed truth and natural religion. The new revelation in Christ, on the other hand, came to a people who had assimilated—however imperfectly—the old covenant. The Old Testament was grafted on to the experience of natural man; the New dispensation was grafted on to the experience of the Old. In the mission to the Gentiles, St. Paul sometimes appeals to men's conscience and to the best in pagan religion; but overwhelmingly his reference is back to the Old Testament. It is tempting to Christian teachers today to take secular man as he is, and ask him to accept Christ as the key to his whole existence, without trying to concern people with the intermediate stage, the Old Testament. In expecting men to jump from natural religion—particularly in its twentieth-century form—to Christ is asking something very difficult: God did not do it this way in history. The least we ought to do is to begin to make Christians more aware of the significance of the Old Testament.

"You did not choose me, but I have chosen you . . ."
If one did not happen to know that these words come from
John 15, one might well have hazarded a guess that they
come from Exodus, Deuteronomy or one of the prophets.
For the basic assertion about the household of God is the
same in the Old Testament as it is in the New. It is not a
man-made society, or a sociological grouping; it is not a
philosophical school, and it is not even a religion in the
ethnic sense: it is a God-made and God-upheld family.

When biblical criticism first came to maturity in the
latter part of the nineteenth century, it was believed that
only after the work of the eighth- and seventh-century
prophets was ethical monotheism breathed into the cultic
and social legislation. To some thinkers this always did
seem too simple a reconstruction. For every one of the
prophets bases his appeal upon certain beliefs which his
hearers were assumed to know about—and believe already
in their heart of hearts. If on the other hand we look at the
religious beliefs of the nineteenth-century scholars, especially the German ones, we find that they possessed a
faith in the supreme value before God of the individual,
which was truly biblical. What they lacked was an equally
profound grasp of the corporate nature of salvation, of
the way in which God uses the divinely-made community.
It followed from this that they severely underestimated the
role of corporate worship, sacrifice, ritual and priesthood,
as vehicles of divine grace and of man's response to God.

In our own day, notable scholars have arisen to redress
the balance. Eichrodt, von Rad, Noth, Eissfeldt, Mowinc-
kel, Albright, Rowley, de Vaux, and many others have
helped to build up a fuller picture. To say that the heart of
the matter is the nation's call in no way demotes the
prophets: they provided the running commentary,

essential for understanding God's revelation through the experiences of his people. Nor if we understand more about the community does it lessen the stature of the individual. Everything that man does, corporately and individually— apart perhaps from breathing and sleeping—has a spiritual coefficient. This is what the call of Israel signifies. All man's actions express his actual valuations; so the obedience to God's kingdom involves the whole of man, and man in society.

The stories of the patriarchs used to be completely written off as folk-explanations of the location of particular tribes, or as legends told at holy shrines. There probably are elements of this kind: for instance Genesis 34 (cf. 49.5) may be a memory of a time when the tribes of Simeon and Levi were settled in the Shechem district—and incidentally these two passages give us a totally different picture of Levi from the ecclesiastical order of later centuries. But a wealth of new information has been gathered, from such Mesopotamian cities as Nuzi, from the Tel-el-amarna letters in Egypt and from Ras-shamra. The patriarchal stories contain many names and customs current in the second half of the second millennium which were not current in later times. So great a mutation in human history as the religion of the Hebrews must have had a historical beginning; and the stories about the patriarchs do contain the seeds of things to come.

We are told how Abraham was *called* by God and how he responded in *faith*. He trekked westwards from Mesopotamia into Syria, and from there into Palestine at the bidding of God. The second millennium B.C. was full of semitic migrations—into Palestine, even into Egypt— what made this particular one such a breakthrough for mankind? Abraham and his descendants traversed un-

known lands and suffered mishaps; yet they went on hearing the *call*. He is to be the father of a great nation whose
existence will affect the whole of mankind for good, "In
thee and in thy seed will all the nations of the earth bless
themselves." Was this an illusion? The one thing that
cannot be denied is that the dream came true.

Abraham was to be the father, not simply of a physical
race of men, but of a genus who would be able to live in
a new spiritual dimension. He himself had to exemplify
this new and highest capacity of the human spirit, personal
trust in the living God, and this we are told he did:
"Abraham believed God and it was counted to him for
righteousness". One cannot even get on a bus without
implicitly trusting the driver; and all the creative partner-
ships in life show what personal faith makes possible. It
is wholly in line with life's total experience that God
should give the greatest prizes to those who enter into a
partnership of faith with him. Abraham's faith is portrayed
in his trek and repeated acceptance of the call, and tested
to the very marrow of human nature in the offering of
Isaac.

If we look at a physical map of Palestine and visualise
the areas settled by the Hebrews in the twelfth century
B.C., the period of the Judges, we can get some idea of the
precarious life they were leading. Here the Bible and
archaeology join hands. The northern tribes are scattered
in the Galilee mountains and in the highlands farther
south round what became Samaria: they are split by the
plain of Esdraelon and the Jezreel valley, a prosperous
belt dotted with strong bronze-age Canaanite cities, armed
with chariots—the ancient equivalent of air supremacy.
Since the Tel-el-amarna period and the decline of
Egyptian power, the Negeb was rapidly returning to

desert conditions, and remained so until the 1950s. The Hebrews were thus clinging to the most inhospitable parts of the country. They were divided by the hostile Canaanites; they were menaced from behind by desert marauders like the Midianites; and last but not least, their existence was threatened by the Aegean invaders whom we call the Philistines. In the couple of centuries that separate Moses and Samuel, what could have preserved the national and religious identity of these tribes but a commonly held conviction about themselves? When we meet them in Palestine they have a national shrine, and a politico-religious confederation that some writers have compared to the Greek amphyctiony of city states. The Hebrews themselves tell us that the thing which really kept them in existence was the knowledge that Jahveh, who had called their distant ancestors, had miraculously brought them out of slavery in Egypt under Moses and made an extraordinary covenant with them. It was made by God himself who is one and unchangeable, and it cannot therefore be overthrown by human circumstances, or even by human sinfulness. So the Book of Judges tells how over and over again the people are practically annihilated, and how repentance brings an immediate divine response in the form of a national leader.

In the second millennium B.C. there were many comings and goings of semitic people to and from Egypt—there may even have been more than one remarkable escape of a group of tribes from tyranny. The crucial importance of the Exodus for Israel lies in the fact that it was seen to be part of a far wider epic. It was the culmination of one stage in the history of God's salvation begun centuries before. Nor does the book of Exodus exalt the providential event above the personal word and revelation of God to

D

Moses. The purpose of the exodus is the new life under covenant.

The purpose of God's choice of Israel and his covenant is set out in words of great meaning and beauty. "You have seen what I did to the Egyptians, and how I bore you on eagles' wings and brought you to myself. Now therefore, if you will obey my voice and keep my covenant, you shall be my own possession among all peoples; for all the earth is mine, and you shall be to me a kingdom of priests and a holy nation." (Exod. 19.4–6 R.S.V.). The whole crucial passage Exodus 19–24 should be studied in this connection. Scholars debate the question, which is the primary concept, the call or the covenant? This will sound to many like a chicken-and-egg argument: what no one doubts is that together these truths constitute the heart of Israel's faith. It is not only the book of Exodus that tells of God's grace and its obligations: the Prophets, the historical books and the Psalms all presuppose it and illustrate it in national and personal life.

Yet the covenant when we come to look at it is a strange kind of bond. Its literary form has been shown to have secular analogies: it is not unlike some documents embodying agreements between Hittite kings and their vassals. But this is worlds away from the Sinai covenant. It is not man who does the giving, but God who gives everything. Man has nothing to do except willingly accept the commandments of God who loves him. Israel was chosen, rescued and endowed by God's sheer grace. "For you are a people holy to the Lord your God; the Lord your God has chosen you to be a people for his own possession, out of all the peoples that are on the face of the earth. It was not because you were more in number than any other people that the Lord set his love upon you and chose

you, for you were the fewest of all peoples; but it is because
the Lord loves you, and is keeping the oath which he
swore to your fathers, that the Lord has brought you out
with a mighty hand, and redeemed you from the house of
bondage . . . Know therefore that the Lord your God is
God, the faithful God who keeps covenant and steadfast
love with those who love him and keep his commandments . . ." (Deut 7.6–9 R.S.V.).

Love is always mysterious. Why does he/she love me?
is an unanswerable question, but the fact of love is true
none the less. The source of the greatest human joy and
creativity is no less real because it is mysterious. So it is
with Israel and the Christian church: its very existence is
due to the mysterious love of God. Bonhoeffer reminds us
that, since it is the church's mission to be broken and scattered and so bear fruit like Christ himself, it is only by the
sheer grace of God that its members even meet for worship and fellowship. How different is the biblical truth
about the church from the cosy-hour kind of religion! It
is utterly different too from the notion that religion is
"helpful" or "inspiring". God's kingdom has either to be
accepted in wondering love, or rejected in favour of man-
made evaluations.

Man-made evaluations of the Old Testament have
abounded in modern times, in philosophy, comparative
history and even theology. The very idea of God choosing
a particular group of human beings for a special privilege
or task was a scandal that had to be brushed aside. The
whole Bible story was rewritten topsy-turvywise, showing
how man discovered God. Now it is true that the kind of
study called the history of religion, *Religionsgeschichte* as
the Germans call it, has produced remarkable results. It
has discovered why primitive men made their myths; it

has shown how religious ideas have developed and cross-fertilised from different cultures. But for the man who actually worships God, this will not do. It is the living God who speaks to *him*, whose grace and demands are found to be unbounded. Some people argue that when you say "Isaiah discovered a new meaning of holiness" you are only saying the same thing as "God revealed a new meaning of holiness to Isaiah". But Isaiah knew what the difference was; and so does anyone else who experiences a moral imperative. One can discover the difference between the two statements also by their fruits. "Isaiah discovered . . ." leads to a wrong assessment of what man can do for himself, to an intellectualist rather than existential picture of religion, and to a purely human opinion as to what matters in life. It leads to an abandonment of faith in the full sense, and it therefore perverts the relationship between God and man. This is the watershed in theology: as Barth has never tired of saying, the Bible is either the word of God or it is the word of man. If we do not take the Bible seriously when it talks about call and grace, we are not likely to take it seriously when it talks about judgement and demands.

One serious handicap to our grasping the full import of biblical truths is the legacy of religious controversy. An observer in Britain in 1650 would probably have seen no viable alternative to some form of Calvinism as the future of English religion. Yet within half a century, this type of theology together with most of the sects had disappeared from the public scene. There were many causes for this remarkable turn of events, but one of them undoubtedly was that men had grown sick and tired of controversies about such matters as predestination. Nor have other forms of the doctrine of *assurance* been free from nauseating smugness. But we ought to take a cool look at the doctrine of election: it is not a Calvinist copyright but a biblical insight.

It is common knowledge that people who lose every vestige of purpose quite literally die. Conversely, the demands of a human situation, someone in trouble, the call of a great leader, the urge to overcome a disability or to break a record—these bring out more than men dreamed they possessed. Extend this truth to the awareness of God's call, and we can see where the dynamics of the spirit will operate. We conventionally speak of engineering and carpentry as *callings*; we usually limit the Christian usage of the word to the ordained ministry or to work in foreign missions. This shows how impoverished our understanding has become. No Christian congregation can be more than a collection of lukewarm well-wishers if it lacks the very thing that caused ancient Israel to exist and survive.

Why was Israel called? Down to 586 B.C. even the prophets seem at first sight to be concerned mainly with the nation's survival, whilst after the exile Ezra and Nehemiah, the later prophets and the Maccabees devote their entire energies to creating an exclusive religion. Not a very outward-looking picture: but neither is the vicar worried to death over the problem of finding a new organist. The problem of survival in the institution is not dissimilar in the two cases, and it is perfectly intelligible. The lack of corporate responsibility amongst the people of God always exacerbates the existing problem of the Church's witness in a sinful world. The Old Testament in fact has a wealth of imagery with which it expresses the intimate life with God to which men are called, and the horizons beyond the present empirical Israel. Israel is to be a nation

of priests. Israel is to know and love Jahveh. Israel is to
walk with Jahveh—the language of the trek to the
promised land is wonderfully elaborated upon. During the
era of the Prophets, the role of the individual is undoubtedly enhanced, but is is done in such a way as not to
weaken the sense of corporate destiny. All through the Old
Testament, the call of the individual prophet or charis-
matic leader and his endowment with the *spirit* of Jahveh
is a microcosm of the call of the nation.

Israel's response is to be expressed in worship and
morality. The notion has been generated that there was
a kind of Catholic versus Protestant feud in Old Testament
times; that priest and prophet were natural enemies
like cat and dog. This is ridiculously unhistorical. Most
of the pioneers of biblical criticism were Liberal Protes-
tants, and though they were men of the highest integrity,
it was inevitable that something of their own attitudes
should have been reflected in their exposition. The
Prophets waged unceasing war against a worship that did
not spring from personal integrity; and sometimes they
came very near to saying that the sacrificial cultus was
not an original part of God's plan (Amos 5.25; Jer. 7.22).
Yet in his invective against false worship, Isaiah includes
prayer—and he can hardly have thought that prayer was
intrinsically bad (Isa. 1.15). Moses, the mediator of the
covenant, is both prophet and priest; so also was Samuel.
There seems often to have been a close relationship between prophet and sanctuary throughout the pre-exilic
period. We cannot assess Hebrew worship simply by
reading the liturgical catalogues in Leviticus: we should
do better to begin with the hymn-book, the Psalms,
which tells us more about the spirit of Old Testament
worship than anything else could. Even the ritual pre-

scriptions are significant, however, for we hear over and
over again the theme that the cultus is to be a token of
Israel's loyalty. The sacrifices with the accompanying
recital of the story of salvation brought Sinai into the
present moment. The covenant lived in Israel's worship:
it was as though they stood at the foot of Sinai and heard
the gracious promises and stern demands. In Joshua 24
we read of one momentous—but probably typical—re-
newal of the covenant. In Deuteronomy 26, the peasant
recites a little creed as he presents his gifts: "A wandering
Aramean was my father; and he went down into Egypt . . .
and the Lord brought us out of Egypt with a mighty hand
and an outstretched arm." The Christian cannot but be
reminded of baptism and the eucharist, where in the
ministry of word and sacrament past and present are
united in the action of the one Lord, the same yesterday,
today and for ever.

The covenant, however, was not only expressed in
worship: the ritual and the civil and ecclesiastical code,
together with the salvation history, was written up in a
series of books called the Law. How does this square
with the assertion that the essence of the covenant is
grace and love? For Wellhausen and his immediate
followers there was no problem, for their axiom was the
Law came *after* the Prophets. But literary scrutiny of Amos,
Hosea and Isaiah with the technique of form criticism
reveals numerous allusions to laws in the Pentateuch.
Some continental Protestant theologians are a little
embarrassed by the fact that the covenant looks on the
face of it so much like a system of imposed legislation.
They tend to look at the Law through the eyes of St. Paul,
and at St. Paul through the eyes of Luther. Jewish
scholars have often urged that St. Paul's strictures on the

Law are not fair; and it must be admitted that because of his Pharisaic background he leaves many Old Testament truths out of sight. But St. Paul apart, there is a very widespread individualistic idea of religion that looks upon laws in the moral sphere as unspiritual. Obedience and duty are curiously contrasted with love. On God's side, however, there can be nothing incompatible with his love in revealing the moral demands of life. "Torah" means something much deeper than law in the secular sense; and "mishpat" not only means a statute, but God's providential and rational government of the universe, in contrast to chaos. On man's side, we get the right approach if we look at Psalm 119: men love the Law because it is a lantern to their feet and a light to their path.

When we look at the history of the Torah *before* rabbinic times, we find that it never was a rigid fossilised system. It was continually developed as the Hebrews met new religious and social problems. Form analysis shows that two quite distinct kinds of legal material have been bonded together in the pentateuch. There is apodeictic law, liturgical and priestly in origin, like "Thou shalt love Jahveh thy God", "Thou shalt not steal". Even this is developed and glossed with theological explanations as God's ultimate demands are referred to particular imperatives. There is also case-law, which must have grown up in real life, as one would expect. A good example is the decisions about injury and compensation in Exodus 21.18–21—this is from the Book of the Covenant, one of the oldest strata in the pentateuch. In Ruth 4 we see the elders at the city gate actually administering and applying covenant law, and here the casuistry would grow.

Moreover it is not suggested in the Old Testament that the Law is too hard to keep. It was only in later rabbinic times that it came to be a labyrinthine system that only the ultra-pious few could hope to obey. All the crucial passages in Exodus and Deuteronomy assume that man's side of the covenant is not too difficult for him. It is not true that the Law is stern and forbidding whilst the Prophets are non-legalistic: it is the Prophets who say that the whole nation except for a remnant will be wiped out for not keeping the covenant.

There can scarcely ever have been a time when the Torah seemed so irrelevant as the present. Has not comparative history shown that all moral rules are relative? Is not the heart of the gospel the very antithesis of law? Paradoxically, there never was a time when men had so many rules to keep as they have now. One can barely take a car on the road without breaking some regulation or other. The fact is that good law is the only thing that can preserve man's freedom. In the case of traffic laws and criminal laws this is obvious; but it is just as true of the personal moral life, and the life of a body of believers. The story of the Protestant community at Taizé is most instructive. This was not an imitation of old-time monasticism: its members found it a sheer necessity to create both a community rule and a liturgy.

When we look at the way in which the Hebrew Law was structured, we can see that its combination of apodeictic and case-law gives us a pattern for a moral theology today. On the one hand, we need clear definitions of the ends of human life as they are seen in God's Kingdom; and on the other hand, we need courageous enquiry into the particular moral stresses to which modern life subjects us.

Other peoples have realised that religion and conduct must go together, that human actions have a right and a wrong that refer beyond what has to do with pleasure or profit. In Hebrew theology, especially under the Prophets, this truth was seen to extend, not only to all human actions, but to human thoughts and motives as well. "It doesn't matter what you believe, it's what you do that counts" is wrong because a man cannot be chopped into two halves—his thoughts on one side and his actions on the other. Every decision and deed and even demeanour expresses the values by which we live. This, incidentally, is why literature is all about morality, even though its devotees often vehemently deny this. For in describing the doings of men and women it is *ipso facto* evaluating their motives. A Hebrew would have also condemned this cliché—"It doesn't matter what you do so long as your heart's right". The Law, the Torah, proclaims that what you do in the factory is as important to God as what you do in the temple; because what you ought to do in the factory is to fulfil the destiny for which God made you. When Matthew Arnold said that "religion is morality tinged with emotion" he was contending, as some men have done right from the Renaissance down to Paul Van Buren, that we can have the values and the moral imperatives without believing in God. It is obviously impossible to disprove this empirically, for all of us know unbelievers whose characters we deeply admire. But a hypothesis like this would have to explain everything in human experience, not just some things; and there are areas of human aspiration and demand that it does not account for.

We must not read the universalism of the gospel into passages where it is not to be found, but there are wide implications right through Israel's story. The covenant with Noah implies certain minimum obligations laid upon all mankind: all men are *de jure* within the Kingdom of

God. That the prophets utter judgements on other nations also implies the responsibility of these peoples. God directs the migrations of peoples: "Are ye not as the children of the Ethiopians unto me? . . . Have not I brought . . . the Philistines from Caphtor, and the Syrians from Kir?" (Amos 9.7.) Micah and Isaiah both contain a passage foretelling that all nations will come in peace to worship at Jerusalem (Isa. 2.2). In Isaiah 60, the heathen nations come as vassals, but the passage is none the less universalistic. Deutero-Isaiah hails Cyrus as Jahveh's anointed one— well knowing that this will shock his Jewish hearers. Jonah is probably a scathing satire on Israel's failure to fulfil its world-wide mission. Finally there is the *servant* of Deutero-Isaiah who sheds his blood in the task of restoring the covenant and enlightening the nations. In assessing the Old Testament we also have to remember what happened: Judaism did become the cradle of Christianity—and of Islam too. Judaism itself has also done something to enrich every culture into which it has grafted itself.

CHAPTER THREE

The Covenant spelt out

The question which exercises the minds of Christians today above all others is belief in God. The *Honest to God* debate brought into the open a deep desire for reassurance and for redefinition. At reading parties at St. Deiniol's Library over the past three years the subjects scheduled ranged from biblical theology to morals and philosophy, but *every time* the discussion came round to belief in God. It cannot be a bad thing that men should be forced back to consider the first principle of their faith. Of how much greater value is this than the weary discussions about vestments and church government! It is by no means irrelevant to the new debate to consider what the Hebrews believed about God: though the important thing is *how* they believed. That they were theists or monotheists may fascinate the historian of religion, but it cannot by itself be of vital concern to us. Nor are we primarily involved in the way their theology developed—that at such and such a date B.C. they became consciously monotheistic. What is most instructive is a thorough understanding of what the life of faith was like for them.

It has often been said that the Hebrews' interest in religion was practical, not speculative. This says too little. There is an absence of metaphysical speculation in the

Greek manner, but it is quite wrong to suppose that the Hebrews had no theology of God. What God does, *that* he is. His metaphysical and moral attributes are deduced from what he is seen to do in Israel's history. Nor were the Old Testament men mere spectators and interpreters: they got their creed from living the life of faith; they were involved in the drama with their whole individual and national life—this is what makes them so interesting to us. People today often speak as though responding existentially to life's demands is the whole of morality and religion. In the Bible, the wholehearted personal response is demanded because of what God is and what he does. Action is no more than instinctive response or blind emotion if it has no facts and reasoning to control its direction.

Practically the whole western philosophical tradition from the ancient Greeks and the Bible agree in believing that behind the flux of life there is a truth that makes sense of it. The early Ionians sought to discover the common substance underlying all nature. Plato wrestled with the relationships between the ideal and the actual, the substance and the individual. British eighteenth-century empiricism was preoccupied with epistemology, the way man knows the world outside. Kant and Hegel tried to work out systems in which the whole of reality can be described in terms of rational principles and processes. Kierkegaard believed that this was starting at the wrong end of the stick—the real datum is man's experience of rational moral choice. But for Kierkegaard as for Tillich in our own day, existentialism is a step towards ontology—spiritual experience leads to knowing God.

On the other hand, the radical German romantics, Fichte and Schopenhauer, and their descendants, Nietzsche

Sartre and Camus, deny the whole premise of Greek
and biblical thought, and allege that there is no given
rational pattern for man to apprehend. For classical
thought the world is a jig-saw that can be put together;
knowledge is the great virtue (cf. Isa. 11.2); knowledge
gives the goal for human life once you have the key; reality
ultimately makes sense. For German romanticism and its
twentieth-century offshoots, *will* is the only real thing;
there is no given order of things; man makes his own values
and goals. Free modern art is the paradigm of this way of
looking at life. There is no external structure to which
man must conform himself. Every law, tradition, religion,
is a series of excuses that man makes up to avoid the fact
of his will. To romanticism nothing surrounds us but the
abyss: we cannot know, we can only will. (I am indebted
to a series of lectures broadcast by Sir Isaiah Berlin
entitled *Some Sources of Romanticism*).

The Old Testament is obviously far closer to Plato and
classical thought than it is to romanticism. There *is* a key
to life—the living God. Creation is a divine order of beings
and functions. History is a purposeful story. Man's freedom
is of the essence of his nature, but it is exercised within the
created order. The goal of nature and history can only be
described in apocalyptic language, but it is still within
the rational framework.

No proof can be offered for the truth of Old Testament
doctrine other than the story and the understanding of it
given by the men themselves. No independent dogma
about the infallibility of the Bible is now available. They
saw the handwriting of the living God: we have to take or
reject their faith. What can be claimed is that the Hebrew
and Jewish religion is basically unlike the other products
of natural religion. If we look at the myth and ritual of

ancient Egypt or Mesopotamia—at that of Sumer, the very matrix of urban civilisation in Asia and Europe— we can see what the standard product was. We can see in these religions how the hopes and fears of men naturally clothed themselves. We can also see in the Old Testament how hard it was for the Hebrews to rise above the standard religion of the day, and to grasp the quite different demands of their own tradition. How did such a faith as theirs come into existence and survive in the millennium and a half from the patriarchs to the Maccabees?

Without the call and the covenant, there would have been no Hebrew religion as we know it. But the Old Testament is not a success story in the human sense. At every point salvation required acceptance and surrender—not a passive state, like baby birds sitting in a nest with their beaks open waiting to be fed, but a role of unbounded national and personal responsibility. God everywhere takes the first step; but Israel comes to know God, and Israel is saved, in the very act of hearing and obeying. In just the same way, Peter and Andrew, James and John, answered Jesus' "Follow me"—and the adventures that followed that decision changed the world. When TV pundits debate the validity of religious truth or the moral problems of theism, they often sound to be talking about something quite different from what the Bible tells us— the experiences of real live men and women.

The story of the Hebrews is full of movement: from Mesopotamia to Canaan, from Canaan to Egypt, from Egypt by way of the Exodus to Canaan again; and finally to exile in Babylon and back again. Not surprisingly, many of the characteristic ways of describing God and his service are derived from journeying. Religion means

walking in the way of the Lord. Judgement is depicted
as a forced march into exile, whilst salvation is a joyful
pilgrimage home to Jerusalem. The Hebrew still called
his house a tent, centuries after he had given up living in
tents. The movable tent is the archetype of the sanctuary
in the Torah—there is no design for a building. This is the
very antithesis of static oriental mysticism. The Bible
knows nothing of genuine prayer that is not linked with
courageous responsibility. Even the *desert* is a symbol of
hopeful journeying, not of flight from the world. "My
presence shall go with you" is the one promise of God that
really counts with Moses (Exod. 33).

It is not surprising that the key words for describing
God come straight from the concrete experience of the
nation and of the individual. When Amos speaks about
God's *righteousness* he means his complete integrity—this
is not only a plumbline which shows up Israel's way-
wardness, it is his absolute faithfulness to his own promises
and his consistency throughout history. The unshakable
love of God is demonstrated for Hosea by his very for-
bearance, the depths of which he infers from his own tragic
experiences. God's holiness for Isaiah is not just the per-
fection of Plotinus' absolute—it is a raging fire that must
purify or destroy every sinful heart. There is the constant
picture of God as judge which reaches its crescendo in
Deutero-Isaiah. History itself is summoned to testify that
God's words are carried out. He is called the God of truth,
not only because he is the source of everything but because
his word is truth, his actions are of absolute consistency. He
is the living God, not only because he is the source of life,
but because he is known in real life.

One of the most instructive episodes is the exile in
Babylon from 586 B.C. to the conquest of Cyrus. Compare

these two passages Ezekiel 8 and Isaiah 40. The former is a flashback to the appalling syncretistic practices in Jerusalem before its fall. The latter is the clarion call at the end of the captivity. Destruction of the national shrine, home-sickness, contact with Babylonian polytheism: which was the most important factor we cannot tell—what is certain is that the Jews were permanently cured of the hankering after the worship of other nations, and the oneness and majesty of God became known as never before. This was the end-product of judgement accepted in the spirit of penitence and faith. But it is naïve to imagine that the tragedy alone produced the faith: little city-states fell by the hundred in the ancient world. The Jewish remnant would not have learned from the exile but for their background of history, commemorative ritual and the schooling of priest and prophet. Religious education has got to be given in every place and with every technique available, to provide the solid foundation upon which meaningful experiences can be built afterwards. The Hebrew tradition was not a fossil but a spark that could set life ablaze at any moment of decision. The prophet drew back the curtain and showed God at work in history; and the Bible and ever-growing tradition of the Church are there to throw a new light on every human situation.

In the Old Testament, men's responses to God are the very stuff of life. It is not for nothing that a version of these words is said at the beginning of Anglican morning prayer: "Oh that today you would hearken to his voice! Harden not your hearts, as at Meribah, as on the day at Massah in the wilderness, when your fathers tested me, and put me to the proof, though they had seen my works." (Ps. 95, cf. Heb. 3.7–11, 4.3–11; Exod. 17.1–7; Num. 20.1–13).

E

Here is the true existentialism, as opposed to the phoney romantic variety: here today, this moment, God calls me to hear and obey. Our choices reveal what we are already. Our choices make us into what we are becoming. To the extent that we are free, we are our own creators. But religion is not concerned with the abstract possibility of free will nor with some amoral life-acceptance. It is not a matter of being constituted in such a way that we can choose between tea or coffee: our choices are tied up with the very deepest values we know—our perception of beauty and ugliness, of truth and falsehood, of right and wrong, and above all with our power to give away our own life for the sake of another. Being face to face with God's choices, to do or not to do is a matter of life and death says Deuteronomy: "I call heaven and earth to witness against you this day, that I have set before you life and death, blessing and curse; therefore choose life, that you and your descendants may live, loving the Lord your God, obeying his voice, and cleaving to him; for that means life to you . . ." (30.19–20 R.S.V.).

If life is like this, it must affect our whole way of looking at history and time; there must be more to it than dates on the calendar or hands on the clock. People today often talk about *the moment of truth*, and this is very close to the biblical way of looking at time. Particular sets of circumstances have a way of revealing a whole predicament for an individual or group. For the Hebrews, the unit of time is the opportunity, the situation created by God, for grace or for judgement. Moreover, the prophets do not think of history as an infinite series or a recurring cycle, but as a drama that is moving towards a climax or *dénouement*. The New Testament takes up this concept of time, *kairos*, and applies it to the coming of Christ and its climax in the passion story. The certainty of the triumph of the Kingdom of God, that nothing is thrown away but every sacrifice is used by God, is the motive-power behind the Old Testament. Must it really be an endemic disease of Christians to live in the past or live on the past? Cannot we even rise to the acumen of the prophets who lived in the present and the future?

That God was Israel's saviour, judge and king meant that he was a freely-acting personal being above nature and history. The rise and fall of dynasties, the movement of the constellations, the migration of peoples and the fertility of the earth are alike under his sovereign will. (Amos. 5.8–9, 9.1ff.; Isa. 40–55.) This would hardly need stressing were it not for the fact that belief in a transcendent personal God is today being called into question—not only by men without religion, but by sincere would-be believers. Nietzsche's silly phrase "God is dead" is taken to mean that belief in a supernatural being is irrelevant to modern man, and that therefore religion ought to be restated in such a way as to avoid the embarrassment of such a notion.

It has already been pointed out that the idea that Israel's tribal god got bigger and bigger needs to be reassessed. Jahveh who brought Israel out of Egypt was at some point identified with the supreme head of the pantheon. This could not have happened gradually— Jahveh either was or he was not lord of gods and men. For belief in such a being was certainly held a millennium before Abraham. The Hebrews knew God as Jahveh who had called the patriarchs and redeemed their descendants from Egypt. There is no convincing reason for denying that this identification goes back at least to Moses. This is the natural interpretation of the Old Testament, and in many cases it makes more sense of the narrative. Elijah's contest with the prophets of Baal is a fatuous affair if it is merely a tussle between two local gods but it looks very different if it has to do with the way in which the supreme being is to be worshipped.

The really decisive thing about God in the Old Testament, however, is not that his name is Jahveh rather than El-baal, but that the Hebrews knew him to be right above nature. "The lions roaring after their prey do seek their meat from God" as the psalmist says, and the spirit, *ruach*, of Jahveh was the breath of all life; but God himself was above and beyond nature. God was even completely independent of the people who knew and worshipped him. In all the other religions of the old world, God and nature were inextricable: the very processes of weather and growth were divine; national territories and national shrines were inseparable from their gods and their honour—gods were almost a blood-relative of their devotees. The irregularities in nature, like storms and floods, were put down to the action of other divine beings. God lived and moved within nature, and so man had to identify himself with his god-in-nature if his crops were to grow and his animals have young. This was what worship was all about. The Christian with his quite different presuppositions finds it hard to realise the motives that lay behind the complex annual fertility ritual. It was all a kind of sympathetic magic, in which man thought he was helping to push round the wheel of nature. Swept along in the sacred dance, lying with the temple prostitute beneath the stars, entranced by the sacrificial smoke rising from the altar, even offering up his firstborn child— man felt himself part of the giant throb of nature.

Only a few decades ago, it was difficult to explain to people what all this was about. Many people thought Stravinsky's *The Rite of Spring* not quite nice when it was first performed. Yet today the "God is dead" brigade tell us that the only hope for the future of religion is to abandon the idea of a transcendent God and to look for purpose only within nature. Would it not be the biggest irony if it turned out that the Hebrews were wrong, and the Canaanites were right all the time! Of course, the radical theologians are not suggesting that we should go back to the fertility myths and ritual. What they mean is that we should look for God, that is, our ideals and satisfaction, within the universe itself. We should find "God" within ourselves by understanding our true nature as moral agents; and we should find him in the situations where man meets man and new depths of experience are struck.

Various forms of pantheism and immanentism are not new. Spinoza attacked supernatural religion, miracles and special revelation and substituted a very persuasive ethic. In the nineteenth century many eminent thinkers were convinced that to think of God as wholly immanent in nature was the only theology that could make sense of the world disclosed by the theory of evolution. Many orthodox Christians in the last century came to realise that the immanence of God as seen in the Bible and the Fathers must be developed alongside other traditional ways of conceiving his action. (Just sixty years ago, in 1907, the Rev. R. J. Campbell put forward his own radical immanentism in a book entitled *The New Theology*!)

We are concerned here with expounding the Old Testament. One of the objections commonly alleged against belief in a transcendent God is that if he intervenes in nature or history at all his action is arbitrary. But this is precisely what the men of the Old Testament did not believe. His mind is beyond human comprehension but he is never capricious: he became known by his very constancy and purposefulness, and by the certainty of his judgement even upon those whom he loved.

The Hebrews appealed to certain facts in their history in support of their belief in a God of supreme power and purpose. When we look back on the whole sweep of their history, even if we are sceptical about some of its details, the persistence of this people coupled with their unique faith presents a remarkable pattern. If we reject the idea of purpose, teleology, on this scale, what is the alternative? The exponents of thoroughgoing immanentism claim that spiritual values are inherent in the universe itself. But does it make sense to speak of purpose in connection with a non-personal entity? Many people want to drop God but retain the *demands* of goodness: but without God, *who* demands?

The prophets reject the idea of arbitrary fate and of capricious gods because they are both too small to account for reality as man apprehends it: ". . . learn not the way of the nations, nor be dismayed at the signs of the heavens: . . . their idols are like scarecrows in a cucumber field . . ." (Jer. 10.2–5 R.S.V.). Yet the Old Testament does not hesitate to attribute human qualities to Jahveh— anger, love, jealousy, sorrow, pleasure. This is by implication a theology of analogy. Man with his spiritual values and freedom is the highest category we know: Israel's creator and redeemer cannot be less than man, he must be personal to the nth degree. The prophets must be taken seriously: they are not the victims of frenzy and hallucination—their inspiration always issues in cogent reasoning. They were talking about God, not about the characteristics of nature or their own psychological satisfaction. There is every reason today to examine the basic difference between natural religion, which shows what man *tends* to believe in, and faith in God who makes demands and will not let man go.

The Old Testament claims that because God stands above the created universe and its history his relation to it is different from that conceived by the nature religions. This is not a question simply of how the world began, but of how man is to live and act as a son in his Father's house.

The earliest of the two creation stories in Genesis 2.4ff. from source J is told in beautiful anthropomorphic words. It is worlds away from the other ancient creation myths with their tales of conflicting gods. Everything centres upon the action of the one creator Jahveh. A Mesopotamian creation and flood story from Nineveh was known to scholars as early as 1872, in which three birds were successively let out of an ark. This was too good to be missed; and from that day on writers have talked about Genesis being derived from *the* Mesopotamian epic—in spite of the enormous theological differences between the two documents. The Babylonian epic in question was not a particularly ancient one, and there were in fact a variety of such stories in Egypt, Canaan and Mesopotamia, differing greatly from one another. There *may* remain a faint memory of the primeval chaos belief in Genesis 1.2; and there *may* be a demythologised allusion to the dividing of the waters in 1.6–9 as also in Psalm 74.13ff. But in most of the ancient stories the dividing of the waters is not connected with the slaying of the monster as in the Gilgamesh.

Some scholarly attention has been focused on the

question: why were such creation stories ever told? They were certainly not framed to give scientific information about the distant past. The primeval age was not thought of as aeons ago—the vistas of paleontology are a very recent possession of man. Creation myths were an attempt to explain the mysteries and paradoxes of man's present condition—good and bad fortune, man's relationship to nature and so on. This should give us a valuable clue to understanding the stories in Genesis: as the Torah and the prophets and the psalms do in different ways, the creation stories embody the basic truths of Israel's creed. Controversies about Genesis and geology and evolution belong to mid-nineteenth-century history: we are concerned with the theological truths in the stories. The compilers of the Pentateuch, in the harvest-time of Jewish thought, wove together the Priestly code with source J and it is quite legitimate for us to take the two creation narratives together in order to see the breadth of their meaning.

God personally creates and sustains all that is. Nature is not a jumble or nightmare but a unitary system with a hierarchy of beings. As Whitehead pointed out, it was no accident that modern science sprang up in Christian lands where this was believed. Nature has such independence as God gives it. Because it is created by his fiat (source P) or by his hands (source J) it operates by definite laws. These laws include the relationships of time and space, the constitution of the particles of matter, and the consequences of human actions.

The created universe is good. There is no dualism at the heart of things; for everything that is can be made to serve God's purposes. These purposes are disclosed in the creation of man as the crown of nature. God's will towards man is wholly good.

Man is made of the dust of the earth and the breath or spirit of God is breathed into him. Here are the two aspects of this "amphibious" creature: he is part of nature in every atom, yet he possesses spiritual autonomy. He is made in the image of God: he can know, will, and create personal relationships with God and his fellows. He can obey, trust and love—and also disobey, betray and hate. A limited dominion is also given to man over the natural world and the creatures in it. Man's ever-increasing power through science is often taken to be a dubious blessing: Genesis has no such qualms. It is unbiblical to speak of any manipulation of the creation as *unnatural* unless it *ipso facto* defeats the spiritual ends of man.

Genesis also tells how, reaching beyond the bounds of his knowledge and conscience, man destroys his innocence. He cannot look at God, and the face of nature turns black towards him. To assess this story, it may be necessary to forget about Milton and the theological edifice built by St. Augustine—they may have been correct, but theirs is not the only possible interpretation.

To begin with, the *fall* story should be read against the background of Israel's undying faith in God as redeemer. Source J is not like Macbeth, where the first temptation leads to ultimate destruction. Nor is the sin of Adam necessarily the outcome of a cosmic drama of fallen angels: the tempter in Genesis is just a clever animal. It is not necessary to suppose that Adam fell from great heights of wisdom and power. It may well be a story of blundering childhood—of innocence so easily lost, as our own generally is. We see a mistake wilfully but so easily made; we see an act of self-seeking that sets up an endless chain of guilt-reactions. This interpretation is not a *tour de force*, it goes back to Irenaeus in the second century—one of

Christendom's greatest seminal thinkers. When Adam and
Eve are seen in really human dimensions, they portray
essential truths about the early history of man, and about
ourselves.

There is a shadow side to the story of mankind, and
there is a shadow side to the story of Israel. But as the
shadow side of mankind leads to the story of salvation, so
the shadow side of Israel brings deeper understanding of
the grace of God. The shadow never blots out the light: the
truths of revelation are seen in sharper relief. Sin and
tragedy brought new situations in which the word of God
was heard. Genesis 3–11 dramatically sets out the deepen-
ing helplessness of the human race, after which comes the
call of Abraham. But tragedy does not end—it is heightened in a sense by the presence of grace, so much is offered, so much is thrown away. The patriarchs and their
descendants are not angels, and the narratives never hide
this. Exodus and Sinai are reached, but this too does not
produce the commonwealth of saints. Someone once wrote,
"How odd of God to choose the Jews!" The chorus of
complaint and despair recorded in Exodus and Numbers
is a bitter commentary on human fecklessness. Every
parish priest has to share something of Moses' pain at the
wicked waste of grace and opportunity—"Forty years long
was I grieved with this generation . . .".

In Canaan the situation was even worse. The late
bronze age civilisation was decaying, but it was far ahead
of anything the Hebrews knew about. There was every
incentive to adopt Canaanite religion along with its agri-
culture and industries. Time and time again the cry of
penitence brought a warrior leader in the nick of time.
This is the recurring theme of the book of Judges. It is

sometimes supposed that repentance and forgiveness do not belong to the Old Testament but only to the New. It is true that in the Torah, apart from the late ritual of the Day of Atonement, there is little in the way of offering for deliberate sin; but one has only to look at the penitential Psalms to realise that divine forgiveness is of the very essence of the old covenant. The prophets and the history books show how this came to be apprehended in the tragic story itself.

Here is something that cannot be explained by psychology or demythologised without destroying it. Repentance and the experience of forgiveness only mean something if a man believes in God who loves and forgives. Otherwise, one does not repent—one despairs and hates oneself, and most of the world's evils can be traced to this very thing. Alternatively, one comes to terms with oneself—evil and all. One cannot restore communion with someone who does not exist.

The eleventh century B.C. brought new hazards. Eastern neighbours like Moab and Ammon made themselves into strong little kingdoms, whilst the Philistines overran Palestine—and, incidentally, gave their name to it. We are so familiar with the story of the capture of the ark of the covenant in the time of Eli, we scarcely realise the calamity of this loss of the national shrine which for centuries had been the nation's rallying point. There was a momentous rebirth of the nation under Saul, David and Solomon, but the shadow never left Israel. From Shiloah to Nebuchadnezzar's destruction of Jerusalem every national hope in the worldly sense was eroded step by step. No tiny kingdom could have withstood a head-on clash with Assyria—scarcely rivalled for cruelty even in the twentieth century. Nor could such a kingdom have survived the game of power-politics between Egypt and Mesopotamia.

When Israel came out of Egypt, a unique privilege was given, and the corresponding responsibility could only have been met by unshakable God-inspired integrity. Such integrity was never there, on the national scale. The betrayal, as the prophets saw it, was threefold. There was the constant tendency to amalgamate Hebrew religion with other cults and to adopt practices, like human sacrifice and ritual prostitution, diametrically opposed to the values of Jahveh's worship. Social evils, which would have broken the hearts of their nomadic ancestors, became endemic. Finally, politics based on the flimsiest opportunism brought together the jaws of the great powers to crush the Hebrew kingdoms out of existence.

"You only have I known of all the families upon earth," says God through Amos, "therefore I will visit upon you all your iniquities." Israel's privilege became Israel's doom. No cynic ever spoke such withering social criticism as the eight- and seventh-century prophets: but they are not pronouncing mere fate. The day of Jahveh must be as black as night (Amos 5.18ff.) and inescapable, but God's purposes did go forward. Hosea came as near as anyone in the Old Testament to saying that God is love, and that his love cannot be defeated. Isaiah sees a purified remnant saved from the fire. Jeremiah, Ezekiel and Deutero-Isaiah all have a message of redemption through suffering.

There is every reason why the people of God today should study the prophets and their message of judgement and redemption. The Church is so ready to complain about the worldliness of the world, so anxious about its own survival. How many sermons we still hear that cite Wilberforce and slave abolition as a proof of Christian action! How little repentance there still is for the three and a half

centuries when Christian nations became rich on the slave
trade, and created race hatred based on colour such as
the world had never known! Nineteen hundred years of
Christian animosity towards the Jews made it possible for
Hitler to massacre six million of them. (A Jew recently
gave me five pounds for our chapel fund: I should like to
meet a Christian who had ever given five pounds to a
synagogue.) The greed and cruelty of the industrial revolution sowed the seeds for communism. In Hosea's phrase,
"You have sown the wind, you shall reap the whirlwind."

Add to this what every Christian knows—the blank
incomprehension and indifference of the masses of
mankind towards the gospel. Christians have to learn from
the prophets what it means to be God's remnant. In Old
Testament theology the remnant does not mean the people
who live to tell the tale. Some of the survivors of 587 B.C.
were unbelievably smug, as we can infer from Ezekiel. Nor
does the remnant consist wholly of those who are known so
to be—Elijah complained in hurt pride that he was the
only faithful Israelite left, and was told by God that he had
seven thousand in Israel who had not bowed the knee to
Baal. The true remnant are those who keep faith. They
accept calamity as part of the reparation for man's sin
against God. When Deutero-Isaiah says "Comfort ye my
people . . . for she has received double for all her sins" he
does not mean that God has had his pound of flesh, but
that the penitent remnant is now to see its faith vindicated
in the release from captivity. The picture of the sufferings
of the servant in Deutero-Isaiah are fulfilled only in the
person of Christ, but the poems also tell us a great deal
about the role of the remnant.

We ought to ask ourselves: In what ways did God work
through the remnant, and in what ways could he do so

now? It is not enough to go on repeating words as though they had some mysterious meaning.

The painful stripping of national pride and the destruction of the body politic forced prophet and priest to look straight at the A B C of their religion, and taught them to treasure what really mattered in it. We can see the sublime outcome of this in the Old Testament. The same could happen to the Christian Church, no longer the privileged religion of the nation, no longer the foremost patron of social welfare—with nothing in its hands but the gospel of Christ. An apparent eclipsing of the status of the clergy could lead to a rediscovery of the role of the whole Church as the royal priesthood.

The Hebrew remnant suffered fear, famine, disease, bereavement and deportation. These evils of themselves have no magical efficacy. "Suffering ennobles" is an absurdly incomplete assertion—it can just as likely twist and destroy men's personalities. We hear much in the Old Testament about the righteous prospering and the wicked suffering; but there is another voice, which we hear particularly in Deutero-Isaiah and Job, which says the righteous do suffer but it is not a meaningless nightmare— God can use even this. The prophets were not foreign correspondents, nor bystanders who say "we told you so": the calamity falls on them too, and they accept it as just because they identify themselves completely with all God's people. They suffered with, and in a real sense they suffered *for*, their brethren. Only by doing this could they minister grace. They became intercessors, pleading with God and pleading with men. The sharing of the nation's guilt and pain fitted the remnant to inspire hope and love. They alone could cleanse the poison of recrimination and break down the barriers between men that guilt heaps up.

Jeremiah, Ezekiel and Deutero-Isaiah show us the work of atonement, of reconciliation between man and God, between man and man, actually being done. Is it really necessary to point the moral for the church's role today?

But, says God to the Servant in Deutero-Isaiah, it is not enough that you should give new life to Israel: you are to be a light to the nations to the ends of the earth. A martyr is not just a sufferer; the word means *witness*. Faithful through pain and rejection, the remnant is to be a permanent witness in the world to God and all he reveals. "You are the salt of the earth . . . You are the light of the world" says Christ to the new remnant. The temptation that Christians should resist today is to become a ghetto, a catacomb, a holy club, a society primarily interested in things like liturgy and introspective prayer. If it does fall into this trap, it will be doing exactly what Judaism did after the return from exile. Judaism forgot about the servant suffering to bring light to the nations and became an exclusive religious enclave. It remained like this until the gospel burst open the chrysalis, as the Lord burst open the sepulchre, and the Spirit drove out the Church to preach to the nations.

Finally, the remnant helps us to comprehend what we may call the *genetics* of salvation. Why was such a unique knowledge of God given to such a small branch of the human family? Part of the answer is that even within that branch, only a small fraction of the population ever seized that revelation with both hands. Take any good cause that requires love and vision: it will be found that it is kept going by a tiny handful of enthusiasts. How could the highest calling of man be expected to work any differently? The prophets and martyrs and saints do mediate truth and power: they alone make it possible for ordinary men and women in each generation to fight the good fight of faith.

The faith of Israel is so much part of our inheritance that it is difficult to see its unique heights. The cardinal doctrine, that God is one, however, is all-demanding. Man's experience of nature did not readily suggest it: day and night and the seasons follow one another, but storms and pestilence do not speak of order and unity. It was an even greater leap to believe in a moral unity, a providential purpose. "Hear, O Israel: the Lord our God is one Lord: and thou shalt love the Lord thy God with all thine heart, and with all thy soul, and with all thy strength." (Deut. 6.4–5.) This is the Shema, the heart of Judaism. It is both the creed and the supreme positive command. People wonder why the Torah speaks of God as "jealous". It is a vivid Hebrew idiom, like Christ's saying that unless a man *hates* father and mother he cannot be a disciple. All the man-ward commandments are summed up in the words "thou shalt love thy neighbour as thyself", but God, because he is one, demands the ultimate and absolute obedience of man. We are continually told today that we should find and serve God in our fellow men, and this is a basic biblical truth, but to make this a complete substitute for deliberate conscious attention to God would have been regarded by the men of the Old Testament and New Testament as blasphemous nonsense.

Man is forbidden to represent God by any outward form: "Thou shalt not make to thyself any graven image." In biblical times, this struck the world as the strangest thing of all about Judaism. When the Bishop of Woolwich tells us that some commonly-accepted mental images of God are wrong, he is echoing the Old Testament; for wrong mental images can be just as misleading and idolat-

rous as those of wood or stone. Great efforts coupled with
the acutest criticism will also have to be put into religious
art, in an age that leans so heavily on visual aids and the
little screen.

All Hebrew theology had a direct connection with real
life; and this is true of the central dogma of God's unity.
The sacred name (Exodus 3.14) is not merely a statement
of God's existence: "I will become what I will become" as
some scholars render it, is a very clumsy expression, but it
shows that Jahveh was understood to be a living, acting,
purposeful being, as opposed to a sublime, wholly other
being. God is one, therefore he whom man trusts today is
identically he who has supported Israel through its
momentous history. Already God could say to Moses "I
am the God of Abraham, Isaac and Jacob"; and this is
the pledge for the future: "I will be with you", "I will go
with you" are constantly heard in the Exodus and Sinai
story. *Immanuel*, "God with us", Isaiah 7 and 8, is the
nation's greatest strength. There is a mysterious presence in
the sanctuary—though Deuteronomy tempers this in
favour of the idea of God's presence in his *word*. Both were
doubtless of great importance; but of even greater significance was the existence of the indestructible community, and the divine presence in the depths of an
individual human soul (e.g. Jer. 1). The presence of the
one almighty could also spell inescapable judgement
(Amos. 9.1ff.); though this very fear could be changed
into loving trust as of a child in its father's arms (Ps. 139).
The eternal unity and integrity of God creates the goal
that his sons are to attain: "For I am the Lord your God;
consecrate yourselves therefore, and be holy, for I am
holy." (Lev. 11.44.)

F

CHAPTER FOUR

The gospels under scrutiny

Call and covenant, judgement and grace, suffering and forgiveness, sacrifice and holiness, the spirit and wisdom— all are spread out before us in the panorama of the Old Testament. In Christ they are all focused into a single point of time and space. But the Church with its faith and New Testament has to live in the modern world with its intellectual and moral upheavals. Since the Renaissance, the New Testament has had a very rough ride indeed and nearly been torn to shreds. Yet despite the massive defection in the Christian nations, the faith has lived. Nor has it survived simply as a nostalgic dream of good old days. When the tale is told, it may well be that more men and women have suffered for Christ in our lifetime under Nazi and Communist persecutions than in any previous age. Christ's living power has been demonstrated, and Christians are coming to look at their Church with eyes wider open—to criticise what is unworthy, and to re-evaluate the gospel. This much must be said at the outset, because we shall have to tread some strange paths in the following two chapters. Here we must look at some episodes in the story of modern biblical study as they directly affect our knowledge of our Lord. In the following chapter we shall set this in the framework of what Christ means to Christians.

Great movements in history have a way of turning into something quite different from what their zealous founders conceived. Such was the fate of the Reformation, as its ideals were overtaken by the Renaissance, and the age of reason succeeded the ages of faith. If Catholic and Protestant nations had gone on massacring one another as they did in the Thirty Years War, they would have consumed each other like the Kilkenny cats—tolerance became a necessity, if not always hailed as a virtue. Many thoughtful men in Protestant lands became nauseated with sectarian controversies. New continents beyond the oceans were opened up, broadening men's imaginations as well as their pockets. A new humanism was well under way before the Reformation began, and this was followed by the most catastrophic breakthrough in all human history, as regards man's relation to nature—the apprehension of the experimental method, which created modern science and technology. The stage was set for a new religion to possess men's minds —only a few brave spirits called it this, but a new set of values and a new conception of the world it indubitably was. Dr. Johnson says that Pope was shocked when someone pointed out to him the implications of his *Essay on Man*: even men who thought themselves traditional believers were seized by the new faith. The challenge of the new picture of the universe to the old was masked for a very long time by the evangelical revival of the eighteenth century, and by the Catholic revival and tremendous religious earnestness of the nineteenth.

Astronomy was not the first science to have the experimental method applied to it, but it was the one which most fired the human imagination in the seventeenth century. The Babylonians and Egyptians had made notable contributions to astronomy: the thing that was new was the hunch that the same laws operate right through the universe, governing the movement of the planets and the fall of an apple, together with the discovery that the earth is not the centre of the universe. These two things coming when they did made a new model for all men's thinking. The universal reign of law must be the expression of God's will. God must either be completely *inside* this kingdom—so said Spinoza the pantheist—or he must be completely *outside* it—as deists said. The model of imposed mechanical law was also extended to the moral sphere. If man could discover the physical laws of the universe, it ought to be possible for him to discover the moral laws that govern his weal and woe. Orthodox Christians replied that it was necessary for God to confirm man's knowledge about right and wrong by means of special revelation; he also had to disclose his threefold nature, so that man could rightly worship him; and he must also disclose the truths about future life. If this does not sound very convincing, it was partly because the theologians of the day had little grasp of the biblical understanding of man's relationship to God.

In this strange debate at the end of the seventeenth century, miracles became a focal point. To the orthodox of the day, miracles were essential to authenticate supernatural revelation. To the deists with their belief in man's power to know the laws of God, miracles were like a red rag to a bull. They developed a two-pronged attack— against the need for revelation, and against the actual occurrence of miracles. Spinoza did this so well that no intelligent modern thinker thereafter could allow himself to think of God tinkering about with the laws of nature (cf. chapter 9). If one were asked to give a single example of man's *coming of age*, no better example than this could be given.

In Britain, the deist attack culminated in Matthew Tindal's *Christianity as Old as the Creation* in 1730, but two further blows were to be struck in 1748. One was an essay by Conyers Middleton in which he argued that the literary remains of the early Christian centuries were wholly in-adequate to back up the claims which Christians made for the New Testament. The other was a highly tendentious essay on miracles by David Hume: one could never obtain sufficient evidence for a miracle, he argued, to overcome the universal presumption of natural uniformity.

The gauntlet was thus thrown down, and Christian scholars had to begin the work of serious historical recon-struction. At first their tools were very clumsy and much of their work sounds unconvincing today: but one small sign of better things to come was Paley's *Horae Paulinae*, which examined some of the internal corroboration of the New Testament. The beginning of the nineteenth century also saw the first weighty English attempt to solve the synoptic problem—an essay by Bishop Marsh. The new century brought the finest techniques of scholarship into play by men of the calibre of Westcott, Lightfoot and Hort. A reasonably accurate text of the New Testament was established, and the majority of the books firmly assigned to the Apostolic age. Meanwhile, Christian belief was being disentangled from the rationalism of the earlier period. Wesley and Coleridge had already fully realised that faith has a grammar of its own; personal religion was deepened by the evangelical movements, and sacramental and mystical piety were developed as a result of the Oxford Movement.

Now we must go back to the age of reason for a moment. If there was no such thing as special revelation, how was the life of Jesus to be explained? Rationalism had to offer a self-consistent alternative to the orthodox Christian view. The first explanation that occurred to the men of those times was that the whole thing was a fraud. The miracles of our Lord's ministry were tricks: when he was supposed to be walking on the sea, he was really standing on a raft; when he fed the multitudes, members of the Essene sect handed out the food from a concealed cave! To crown it all, his disciples stole his body after the crucifixion and gave it out that he had risen from the dead. Views of this kind were published in Britain between 1727–29 by Thomas Woolston, and were being repeated in modified forms by German scholars practically to the end of the eighteenth century. Now whatever our ultimate response to the gospel may be, one thing is psychologically impossible to believe: that the men of the New Testament were scoundrels. The *fraud* theories died a natural death; but thus began what has come to be known—from the English title of Schweitzer's book—as "The quest of the historical Jesus".

More serious trials were on the way. At the beginning of the nineteenth century, great strides were made in the study of the history of ancient Greece and Rome. It was found that, if the stories about the gods were deleted from the ancient authors, and a number of incidents reinterpreted, a credible narrative could be pieced together. It was inevitable that the same method should come to be applied to the Bible. Moreover, stories of the marvellous follow the saint like seagulls follow a ship. St. Francis Xavier wept over his difficulties in communicating with eastern peoples; yet within a generation of his death he was being credited with the gift of tongues. Another factor is the uncertain authorship of ancient books. A book purporting to be the meditations of King Charles I circulated for several decades—whilst the facts about the book were also in print! All this produced what has come to be called the *mythical* explanation of the gospels which reached its highwater mark in D. F. Strauss' first *Life of Jesus* of 1835. The book was translated into English by the young George Eliot, and permanently affected her beliefs and the lives of many free-thinkers. Strauss argued that, within a generation, the Galilean prophet had been transformed into a saviour-god. He thought that one could actually see the myth-making process within the New Testament.

Many orthodox scholars refused to shelter behind the doctrine of biblical inspiration, and sought to carry the war into the enemy camp. The very year that Strauss published his first *Life of Jesus*, Lachmann made known his findings about the synoptic problem. There is obviously some literary connection between Matthew, Mark and Luke, and various hypotheses had been put forward to explain it. Lachmann's hypothesis, that Mark came first and was then used independently by Matthew and Luke, opened up a new era of creative New Testament study. The gospels came to be set firmly within the first century, and many early rationalistic theories were shown to be flimsy— Strauss, for instance, had argued that we can see the heightening of the miraculous from Matthew through Luke to Mark!

Strauss' main thesis, however, that the story of Jesus had undergone a metamorphosis, did not die. Darwinian evolution gave a new impetus to a genetic view of history that had been gaining ground for some time. The human story was a seamless garment, woven from the interaction of natural forces. It should be added that as time has gone on, the organic view of history has had to be drastically modified, and twentieth-century historians are much less prone to talk about *laws* of history; for tiny individual circumstances can affect the fortune of empires—like the shape of Cleopatra's nose, to cite J. B. Bury's celebrated example. Philosophers of history like Dilthey, Croce and Collingwood, have greatly rehabilitated the importance of the individual person and the uniquely fertile situation. Nevertheless, when history is thought of as a continuous web of natural causes and effects, this not only *de facto* rules out sudden divine intervention, it also comes to be extended to the realm of ideas, which are thought to develop as an unbroken process. Thus, when a particular religious belief is examined, the question is asked, what were its antecedents, and what human needs was it thought to meet?

In German Protestant theology Strauss and his immediate successors were not looked upon altogether unfavourably; for attention was now being focused upon the teaching of Jesus rather than upon the church's dogmas about him. The stripping-off of the mythical and miraculous elements in the gospels, it was thought, could only enhance the significance of Jesus' words and human example. The age which believed progress, material and moral, to be of the nature of our existence found it most congenial to approach religious truth in this way. Jesus was thought to have taught a pure doctrine of the fatherhood of God and the brotherhood of man. The Kingdom of God was thought to mean the reign of love and justice brought about by the enlightenment of mankind. After the horrors of the twentieth century, it is difficult to think oneself back into the world of a century ago. Men at that time differed profoundly in their beliefs about whether Jesus performed miracles and rose from the dead, but they were at one in hearing our Lord's words as chiming in with their beliefs about the future of mankind. We can be pardoned for envying them.

We are concerned here with this approach only in so far as it affects the method of New Testament study—we shall return to the doctrinal considerations in the following chapter. As time went on, it became increasingly hard to keep up the *liberal* interpretation of Jesus without doing violence to the evidence. Many of Jesus' sayings are linked up with incidents of an apparently miraculous character: how can we speak of the words being authentic and not the deeds? Then again, is Jesus first and foremost a teacher of human ideals? There are the prominent exorcisms, and the teaching about judgement, heaven and hell. The parables and stern words to the disciples could be allegorised into something akin to Kant's categorical imperative. What refused to be demythologised in this way was rejected as an encrustation of Jewish ideas.

One interesting example is afforded by Wilhelm Wrede, whose views still find adherents. Jesus never claimed to be Messiah, it is said; and to cover up this embarrassing fact, the writer of St. Mark's gospel invented the idea that Jesus kept his Messiahship a secret. It is surprising how little imagination some scholars have: for if Jesus was not to cause a blood-bath, the one word he could never have uttered in public was *Messiah*. John 6.15 recalls what could have turned into a very ugly incident. Scholars continued to go to great lengths to minimise all that was Jewish, national, supernatural and dogmatic in the gospels. The message about Christ must be universalised, the mistake was to try to do this before all the historic facts were properly understood.

The thing which put a cruel end to the older liberal theology was the study of Jewish non-biblical literature from the hellenistic period. This was the milieu of Jesus and his disciples and it could not be ignored. Johannes Weiss and Albert Schweitzer horrified their contemporaries by claiming that what had previously been thrown out as Jewish accretion was actually the heart of Jesus' view of things.

What Schweitzer said was roughly this: Jesus' ethical teaching was not intended to be moral philosophy for an enduring civilisation: it was the precipitate action demanded of men who knew that the present world order was shortly to come to an end. God is to burst into our world with judgement and salvation; therefore sell up—turn the other cheek—live for today like the wild birds. Jesus expected that his preaching would herald God's intervention. He kept on expecting it: he thought it would happen before the twelve got back from their preaching tour (Matt. 10). He then went to Jerusalem for a final show-down, certain that God would vindicate him in the hour of suffering. God did not do this, and he died with a broken heart, all his dreams shattered.

Schweitzer tampered with the gospel evidence, for he believed his thesis to be irrefutable. For instance, his assertion that Jesus expected the end to come during the mission tour rests on the assumption that Matthew 10.23 ("Ye shall not have gone through the cities of Israel, till the son of man be come") was spoken in the circumstances described in Mark 6.7. But Matthew 10, like Matthew 13, 18 and 25, is a series of non-Marcan sayings fitted into a Marcan situation; and there is no presumption that these sayings were uttered in the Marcan situations. Nevertheless, Weiss and Schweitzer had put their finger right on the central point of Jesus' teaching: what Jesus was talking about was the kingdom of God, not the kingdom of man

Once this fact was grasped, nothing could put the old Humpty-Dumpty together again.

Schweitzer's challenge could not be met by holding up hands in horror. Too much was now known about Jewish thought in New Testament times for it to be plausible any longer to cut out every reference to the supernatural in our Lord's words. The only way forward was to examine the new insights more profoundly. The man whose name will for ever be associated with the next step forward is C. H. Dodd. He began by taking a fresh look at the parables. A German scholar named Julicher had already broken new ground by showing that the parables are a distinct form of teaching. Each describes a real situation in nature or human affairs which reveals a single truth about the kingdom of God. Older exegesis had treated the parables as inexhaustible allegories—the Good Samaritan's innkeeper, for example, might be the pope; the two pence, the two gospel sacraments. Today, it is beginning to be seen that the attempt by Julicher, Dodd and Jeremias to cut out allegory altogether will not hold; because the men of the New Testament lived in a thought-world that worked by typological imagery. But at the time that Dodd did his early work, the stripping-down of the parables brought daylight into a very difficult crisis for theology.

Dodd saw that the parables are predominantly about the *present* not the future. The Kingdom *has* come; judgement and mercy *have* come in the very person of Jesus. The bridegroom is come; the thief in the night is here; the king has got back suddenly. Even the dishonest steward knows that the moment of truth has come, whereas the official representatives of God's people cannot see the *signs of the time* staring them in the face. Men must now accept or reject salvation as they are confronted by it in Christ.

Schweitzer had maintained that Jesus spoke of a *future* act of God: Dodd tried to cut the ground from under Schweitzer's feet by showing that much of Jesus' teaching is about God's action in the *present*. Dodd went on from what he had said in *Parables of the Kingdom* to show in *The Apostolic Preaching* that essentially the same message runs right through the New Testament. Whether we look at the speeches in Acts, the epistles or the gospels, we find the same pattern: the proclamation, kerygma, which the Apostolic Church brought to the world was that God had acted decisively in Jesus Christ; that in him the kingdom was fulfilled; and that this was demonstrated by his dying and rising and by the outpouring of the Spirit.

This way of looking at the New Testament which came to be known as *realised eschatology* has had to be slightly modified; for deep in the gospels there is an inescapable reference to a future consummation of the Kingdom. Jesus says, "The Kingdom of God is *entos humon*" which means within you, or among you; yet he teaches his disciples to pray "Thy kingdom come". This paradox reflects the facts as we know them. The first disciples knew that the kingdom had come in Jesus—this was the heart of their faith. But the world as they looked out on it—and as we look out on it—seems very far from the Kingdom. Like the men of the New Testament we are bound to look for a completion of what has been so gloriously begun.

The more radical type of gospel criticism has of course gone on developing in the twentieth century. Strauss was one of the forerunners of the history of religion method. Another landmark was a book named *Kyrios Christos* by a German named Bousset in 1907. Alexander the Great's empire collapsed politically after his death, but culturally it went on expanding, and became what we call

the hellenistic world—to distinguish it from Hellenic, that
is, Greek culture. In the new hellenistic Mediterranean
world, Greek civilisation travelled eastwards and oriental
ideas moved westwards. The mystery religions were a
typical blending of eastern and western ideas. It is easy
enough to point to half a dozen superficial resemblances
between mid-first-century Christianity and the mystery
religions: initiation symbolising dying and rising with the
hero-god, a sacred meal in which the hero-god's life is
partaken of, and above all, the idea of the hero-god himself. Bousset argued that the jump from the Jewish prophet
and his disciples to the hero-god and his worshippers took
place at Antioch, where Christianity passed from Jewish
into dominantly Gentile hands.

Christians should not pooh-pooh this reconstruction,
destructive though it sounds. The person and work of
Christ underwent successive stages of interpretation.
No one, for example, would claim that the Athanasian and
Nicene creeds are contained word for word in the New
Testament—fundamentally congruent though they may
be. We can actually see in the New Testament itself different stages in the presentation of the gospel. If we look at
the speeches represented in Acts 2–13 the theme is that
Jesus, though rejected and crucified, has been declared by
God to be Messiah by raising him from the dead and
exalting him to his right hand. The epistles of St. Paul, the
epistle to the Hebrews and the prologue to the fourth
gospel give far wider interpretations of Jesus' mission. The
question is not whether there is fresh interpretation, but
whether it is right interpretation.

Bousset's claim that the gospel was turned into a hellenistic mystery religion at Antioch is a misrepresentation.
St. Paul sometimes uses the jargon of astrology, and he

uses religious words which were common in the ancient world. But he could never have been present at a mystery rite, and would have known no more about them than the man in the street knows about what happens at a masonic lodge. But he did know that hellenistic religious language reflected the deepest yearnings of men—and to these he appealed. The New Testament beliefs about Jesus and salvation are radically different from the mysteries at many crucial points. Moreover, the New Testament concepts of Christ's person are based on Jewish, not Gentile, ideas. Jesus as victorious Messiah and Lord is portrayed in the words of Psalm 110.1—probably the most oft-cited Old Testament passage in the New Testament. Philippians 2. 5–11 and Hebrews 1, which express the most advanced Christology in the New Testament, are completely Jewish in character, blending Old Testament truths in a unique way. Members of the history of religion school today are admitting that the crucial formative period of Christology was the two decades after the crucifixion, and in Palestine. The interval between Christ's earthly life and the writing of 1 Corinthians is no longer than from the middle of the last war until now.

We saw that as far back as 1835, Lachmann proposed the priority of Mark as the solution of the *synoptic problem.* There is a further body of material common to Matthew and Luke which is not found in Mark. From the way in which Matthew and Luke make use of Mark, it has been inferred that they used a second source—perhaps it was no more than a collection of Jesus' sayings—to which the symbol Q is attached. Several writers since the war have unsuccessfully tried to advance an alternative—that Luke simply used Mark and Matthew. If Luke knew Matthew, why use Mark—and why have taken so many sayings out of their contexts in Matthew and invented quite new situations for them? An effigy of Q was ceremonially burned in the quadrangle of Keble college several years ago—unfortunately, enthusiasm is no substitute for hard thinking.

After the first world war, the gospels came to be studied in another way, which was called form criticism, *Formsgeschichte*. If we take a passage like Mark 2.23–28, Jesus in the cornfields, we have an incident that might have happened on any spring-time sabbath during the ministry. It is like a modern line-drawing—every irrelevant detail is rubbed out; the story is told for the sole purpose of giving the setting to a saying of Jesus. Sayings often appear in groups, joined either by a common word or similar theme. Parables and miracle stories have each their own succinct character. In our age of abundant printed matter, it is difficult to grasp the extent to which men's memories were trained in the old world: learning by heart was systematically practised to a degree impossible to us. Material was arranged so as to facilitate learning. Centuries of rabbinic teaching already lay behind when Jesus taught his disciples. St. Mark's gospel was probably not written until 35 years after the Ascension: in this interval, the message was being continuously preached and the material further crystallised—not only for memory's sake, but into forms which clearly brought out the meaning of what Jesus said and did. Our gospels thus represent not the isolated testimony of this or that apostle but the commonly accepted tradition of the believing church.

The gospel writers, however, did not simply string together these already finely cut gems of the tradition; they each work out a portrait of Jesus subtly constructed by selecting and arranging the tradition. A good illustration is the different ways in which Matthew and Luke use the

little group of sayings about discipleship. St. Mark tells
how the disciples bundle Jesus into a boat and set out
across the lake. Matthew makes the scene look quite different. First, he puts the Lord's words about the absolute
demands of faith (8.18ff.), then he goes into the boat and
the disciples *follow*. Thus by word and action Matthew
illustrates the kind of practical commitment that Jesus
demands in his church. A literary artist like Luke would
not have dismembered a sequence like this if it had been
in his source. In fact he has his own meaningful place for
the sayings about discipleship. In 9.51 begins the long
section representing our Lord's journey to Jerusalem and
the Passion. The hinge of the story at this point is Mark's,
but the drama is heightened by the length of the journey
period. It is at the outset of this way to the Cross—which
the disciple must share—that Luke places "Foxes have
holes" and "Leave the dead to bury their dead" (9.57ff.).

The gospels are not biographies in the modern sense;
they are bare of the kind of information about our Lord
that we should dearly love to have. They are theological
books, interested only in the supreme act of salvation
wrought by God in Jesus. Everything in the gospels is
there because it was believed to witness to the basic kerygma. The oral tradition from which the writers drew was
like this also. A saying or incident would be treasured if it
was seen to have a bearing on Christ's saving work, and a
relevance to the Christian individual and community here
and now. As we penetrate through the New Testament into
the life of the first Christian communities, we see the mainspring of their existence. The Lord who had healed the
sick, preached the coming of the Kingdom, been crucified
and raised, was the very Lord they worshipped now and
followed in their lives. Every detail that mattered about

Jesus' teaching and passion was told and retold because it painted the picture of the living Lord. It is obvious that the Church and the gospel writers selected their materials: the question now is did they *modify* or even *fabricate* their materials? In the past quarter of a century, scholars— especially those who have leaned on form criticism—have tended more and more to think that this is what happened. We can take any incident in the gospels, and without the slightest difficulty we can see what it must have meant to the Apostolic Church. Increasingly it has come to be assumed that this counts against the historicity of it. A careful reading of the Pelican commentary on St. Mark will reveal the process at work. Professor A. T. Hanson and his friends have made a spirited attack upon this presumption of unhistoricity derived from form criticism in the volume entitled *Vindications*. On the other side, it is argued that it does not really matter for Christian faith if many of the incidents in the gospels are fictitious, because they still witness to the depth of the Early Church's faith in Jesus. The very existence of the Church with its faith and spiritual power is the real evidence for the truth of it all, says Professor J. Knox in his *Church and the Reality of Christ*. It is doubtful whether many Christians will be content to rest in such a position: if the primitive Church cannot be trusted to tell the words and deeds of Jesus, how can it be relied on for its doctrine? Bultmann was prepared to say that we can know very little indeed about the man Jesus— what matters, he says, is the reality of faith in God's grace and the door which it opens to authentic living. But it is significant that some of his pupils are trying very hard to pick their way cautiously back to a more positive view of the gospels and of the role of Jesus in the creation of the Christian religion.

G

The position within the history of religion school regarding the New Testament is well illustrated by R. H. Fuller's recent book *The Foundations of New Testament Christology*. The terms for describing the person and work of Christ, he says, passed through three stages. Jesus believed himself to be the prophet of the end-time, through whose sufferings the promised kingdom of God would become a reality. Aramaic-speaking disciples then interpreted his mission in the light of their certainty that he had overcome death. They identified him as the Davidic Messiah, the Suffering Servant of Isaiah 53, and the exalted Son of Man of Daniel 7. Jewish Christians familiar with the Greek Old Testament then carried all this a stage further. From passages like Psalm 110.1—where *kyrios* is used both for Jahveh and his Messiah—they built a two-stage Christology. We can see this in the speeches in Acts and the introduction to the epistle to the Romans: a human, suffering Messiah is afterwards exalted to the right hand of God and given the name *Lord*. Finally, Jewish Christians with a strong hellenistic milieu created a three-stage Christology: the pre-existence of the Son, or Word; his incarnation and humiliation; and finally his exaltation (cf. John 1.1–14; Heb. 1; Phil. 2.5–11; and Col. 1).

To anyone unacquainted with the story of biblical criticism, this must seem a very bleak place to have reached. But when we compare it with the kind of thing that Bousset wrote sixty years ago, there is very substantial progress. The notion that the decisive interpretations of Christ took place when the gospel passed from Jewish into predominantly Gentile hands is now untenable. According to Fuller, the crucial steps were taken before this happened, amongst Jewish disciples. The words that embody the highest conceptions of New Testament Christology were on the lips of these disciples. The time-scale in which this came about is also significantly foreshortened.

This throws light on another serious problem that has dogged New Testament studies for a hundred years. The Tübingen scholar, F. C. Bauer, maintained that in the Apostolic age there were two radically opposed versions of Christianity. There was a Jewish and more original version of the gospel, that stood for a wholehearted rabbinic orthodoxy plus the belief that Jesus had been the expected Messiah; and there was the Christianity of Paul, with its rejection of the Law, and belief in a world-wide mission to the gentiles. One of Bauer's planks was a late second-century book known as the *Clementine Recognition*—which scholars today would not rate higher than a historical romance emanating from a Judaeo-Christian breakaway sect. In this work, James of Jerusalem is represented as a sort of super-Pharisee, a man who would have been a natural antagonist of St. Paul. To prefer the pseudo-Clementines to the contemporary first-hand evidence of the epistle to the Galatians is to prostitute the study of history. A controversy there undoubtedly was, and St. Paul makes no bones about it; but it concerned the question whether Gentile Christians ought to keep the Jewish ceremonial law—this was a heart-rending problem for some Jewish Christians, it was not a smokescreen to hide a fundamental disagreement about the gospel. When we compare the New Testament documents, there are the strongest reasons for believing that there was free intercourse of theological ideas between St. Paul and the mother churches of Palestine.

If we think of the very early date when the epistles to Rome, Corinth and Galatia were written—the authenticity of which even Mr. Morton and his computer cannot

deny—we have within little more than a couple of decades
of the death of Christ a Christology that includes at least
these elements: Christ is the incarnation of the pre-existent
Son through whom all things were created; his humiliation
and death is described as a divinely appointed expiation
for the sin of mankind; he is the Davidic Messiah who is
now the exalted Lord through whom the faithful, at his
coming, will be transformed or raised from the dead.

Even according to the radical criticism of our day, therefore, the narrowest gulf divides the master from this
elaborate theology based on the conjunction of Old Testament symbols. Is the crevasse really too wide to jump
across? Dodd wrote a most interesting book on the use of
the Old Testament in the New, *According to the Scriptures*,
at the end of which he confesses that we must postulate a
uniquely creative mind to have seen and worked together
such different themes. Is it so unreasonable to believe that
Jesus played as great a part in the creation of Christian
thought as Luther did for the Reformation or Marx
for communism? To minimise the role of individual
minds as the history of religion school has so often done and
to talk about *forces* and *milieux* is not even in line with the
best secular historiography of our century.

Supposing we had had the privilege of working during
the second world war with a great leader, and shared his
mind in grappling with daily problems for a year or more,
we should most certainly have discussed every burning
question of the day with him, and it is equally certain that
by now we should still be able to remember what he had
said. It is admitted that Jesus proclaimed the kingdom of
God, the fulfilment of history, in which his own sufferings
were to play a decisive role: by what possible objective
canon can it be argued that his authentic voice stops here

and that we know nothing of his views about anything else?

Even if it were granted as a matter of historical probability that all the theology of the New Testament came straight from the mind of Jesus, this would still not prove it to be true. It might all be a dream in his mind, the most sublime moral and metaphysical vision of all time. But then, we are in just the same position as Peter and Andrew, James and John: we have to follow him to see whether the vision measures up to the heights and depths of human experience.

CHAPTER FIVE

God in Manhood

We must now set the quest of the historical Jesus against a much wider background. Much of what has looked so barren may turn out to have lively implications for the Christian's life. Many thinking people must be vaguely aware that the Lord in whom they believe is depicted very differently today from the Christ of previous ages. Those with an O-level standard of Religious Knowledge realise that modern biblical criticism brings its own perspective to the life of Jesus. Few, however, could put their finger on the crucial changes, and few even of the experts take the trouble to look at the changes in the whole context of Christian history.

In the third, fourth and fifth centuries, the schools of Alexandria and Antioch had distinctive ways of looking at the person of our Lord as well as their different approaches to the study of the Bible. The Alexandrians were primarily concerned with the way in which God saves us by taking *representative* manhood into himself in Christ. Man's nature is not inimical to God, for it was made in his image, and but for sin would have continued to enjoy uninterrupted communion with him. Men who are incorporated into Christ by baptism and fed by the eucharist have their human nature made in a real sense divine. This is not unscriptural. Anyone who reads Dr. J. A. T. Robinson's short book *The Body* can see how realistically St. Paul took his belief in salvation by incorporation into Christ. Indeed, in some respects the Alexandrian theologians were very true to the New Testament kerygma.

The Antiochene school, as we saw in the first chapter, was firmly wedded to a literal interpretation of the gospels, and with this went a sharper perception of our Lord's human life. This in turn accentuated the question of the relationship between Jesus' manhood and deity. The theologians of Antioch tended to adopt what we should call psychological descriptions of the unity of God and man in Christ.

The ecumenical council of Chalcedon in A.D. 451 issued a carefully thought-out communiqué, which was used as a standard of reference in all the main Christian churches down to the end of the nineteenth century. It safeguards—as far as a formal statement like this can do— the true deity and true manhood in Christ; but it cannot be denied that the Christ as he was worshipped in patristic times was predominantly a figure of awesome majesty. The glorious Byzantine mosaics characteristically depict Christ as the heavenly ruler and judge. The Lord's Supper became an awesome mystery—consecrated behind the closed doors of the iconostasis in the east or by the silent words of the Latin canon in the west. Our Lady and the saints became the *de facto* mediators between God and men.

A great change came about with St. Bernard (d. 1153). His hymn "Jesu, the very thought of thee", gives some idea of his new approach to our Lord's person. As well as being the divine Son and judge, he could be known and loved through his manhood. From St. Bernard's time onwards,

our Lord's very body, made of our flesh and blood, became
the object of the most poignant love. Devotion to the cruci-
fix, the five wounds and the precious blood; exercises like
the Stations of the Cross and the rosary—all these quickly
sprang into prominence as expressions of worship through
Christ's manhood. To many of those brought up outside
the Latin tradition some of these devotions seem mawkish,
but at heart they are truly evangelical, because they
represent an irresistible Christian urge to get close to the
real live Jesus of the gospels. How irresistible it is can be
seen from the fact that although the Reformation snuffed
out the outward expressions—the statues and pictures and
popular prayers—devotion to the Passion and precious
blood came back like a tidal wave in the eighteenth century in Charles Wesley's hymns. The human Jesus had
been born again in the Christian imagination in the days
of St. Bernard; and the ice age that followed the Reformation could not for ever repress the expression of this in
worship. Jesus is loved in his pain and sorrow because he
is the compassion of God for us. God *so* loved the world:
we see God himself in everything that our Lord was and
did; and loving our Lord as man is a perfectly reasonable
response.

Some voices within Lutheranism in our day have denied
this. Nygren, in his *Agape and Eros*, argues that God's love
for us is "uncaused love"—he makes his sun to shine on the
just and unjust. We are commanded to love our neighbour
with a love analogous to this. Our only proper attitude
towards God is faith. If we introduce the idea of loving God
with our emotions we are back, Nygren says, to St. Augustine, who misleadingly combined the New Testament
agape with the Greek *eros*—we are back to a sub-Christian
idea of loving what delights our mind and feelings. The

most penetrating reply to this was made by J. Burnaby in a study of St. Augustine called *Amor Dei*. Can we really suppose, he contends, that Peter and John and Mary Magdalene were not drawn to Jesus by a love which included natural feelings? *Philia* and its cognates is the name for this kind of love, which cannot be eradicated from the New Testament. It is as natural for a man to love Jesus as it is to love his best earthly friends.

One aspect of our Lord's incarnate life neither St. Bernard nor Charles Wesley could have come to grips with. A peculiar condition of human life is that we live on a pin-point of time. The present is gone into the unalterable past in a flash, and the next instant is totally unknown. This fact is normally blurred because our memory stretches out behind us and our imagination reaches out in front of us. But it is still the pin-point of our experience that gives our life its peculiar quality. Our hopes and fears, our longings and regrets, the pain of separation and the joy of reunion—all arise from our living in a moment of time. However much a life is under-pinned by faith it still has this characteristic. Could it be that Jesus shared our experience to the extent of living himself on the pin-point of time? As long as the framework built up by the Fathers was looked upon as the only legitimate reference for interpreting the gospels, the question could not be raised. The metaphysical attributes of God the Son—including his omnipotence and omniscience—were thought to be possessed by Christ, who in becoming man had added another nature without diminishing his Godhead. The sacred humanity of Christ had its soul, or principle of natural organisation, and its own will, thought of as a kind of faculty. But the manhood was impersonal, in the sense that the "I" who knew and spoke was God the Son. Christ's knowledge and power were thus absolute: his teaching was God's own voice; he had power over loaves and fishes and storms; he could have summoned twelve legions of angels to his aid.

Today one scarcely opens a book dealing however incidentally with the life of Jesus which does not take it for granted that he shared our experience of living in the passing moment. It is assumed that he shared our limited knowledge of the future and our restricted information about the present. Here is one of the greatest revolutions in Christian thinking that has ever taken place. How did this change come about? We have already traversed much of the ground in the previous chapter. When we looked at the quest of the historical Jesus, we saw that as time went on more sophisticated historical techniques were used. For a long time, the quest hardly affected orthodox thinking about Christ's person. It was regarded as an intellectual game by unbelievers trying to justify their faithlessness— important indeed to apologists but of little concern to the dogmatic theologian. Dr. Pusey was one of the very few British theologians who knew what was going on in the German universities, and he was scarcely impressed. Ignorance and indifference in Roman Catholic academies was even greater, with a few shining exceptions like Dr. Döllinger. But as the nineteenth century proceeded, reputable orthodox theologians began seriously to use the tools of historical criticism. We have already mentioned the work of Westcott (d.1901), Lightfoot (d.1889), and Hort (d.1892), who did so much to reveal the true historic foundations of Christianity. But the process could not stop short of looking at the contents of the gospels with the eyes of a historian. The historian wants to know what a situation looked like to men who were caught up in it; and he tries to see whether a person's words and deeds reveal a significant character—a person whose thoughts and motives can be intelligibly discussed.

Just over a hundred years ago, in 1866, an eminent Cambridge historian, Sir John Seeley, published (anonymously) a book entitled *Ecce Homo*. It was a life of Jesus with a difference. Seeley attempted the difficult task of looking behind the Gospel story to the mind of Jesus himself. Picture our Lord at the moment of his baptism, aware of his inner union with God, aware of the power of the Spirit flowing through him. What was he to do? How was such a ministry to be exercised? In the story of the temptations, we see him wrestling with this problem—if no human mind is at work, says Seeley, these stories are meaningless. But we do in fact see Jesus wrestling with the problem how rightly power is to be used, and the miracle of the whole gospel story is not the presence of power but the control of it.

Thus Seeley sought to give a meaning to our Lord's life by setting it squarely within the problem that has vexed mankind from Prometheus to the H-bomb. Many people will not agree with this reconstruction. Seeley had little understanding of the eschatology of the gospels: on the saying about baptism with fire, he makes a remark about moral warmth! But the point is that a psychologically intelligible picture of Jesus was being sought—and sought by someone who had no rationalistic axe to grind.

The final controversy in this country over our Lord's human mind was a storm in a theological teacup. Strange it is that so momentous a matter should have caused so little interest outside academic circles. The question cropped up in a rather odd way. Towards the end of the last century, some of the broad conclusions of biblical criticism were rapidly gaining ground—the four-source theory of the Pentateuch, the non-Davidic authorship of the Psalms, and the Maccabean dating of Daniel. A number of very conservative scholars led by Dr. Darwell Stone contended that these questions are closed to us because of Jesus' authoritative words: he cites Psalm 110 as being by David, and regularly alludes to the Pentateuch as Mosaic. Gore, in his essay in *Lux Mundi* in 1889, followed up with his Bampton Lectures and volume of dissertations, denied this conclusion. He suggested that it was part of our Lord's incarnate condition to share the limitations of human knowledge.

Once this idea had been openly mooted—and by a high churchman of such eminence as Gore—the new approach to the gospels and a new kind of Christology spread rapidly: it was as though men had been waiting for someone to give the signal. Books began to appear with titles like *Studies of the Mind in Christ*, and *Studies in the Inner Life of Jesus*: at long last, it was believed, Jesus could be thought of as a real man and his mind and motives discussed. Some of this reconstruction—like that of the German Ritschlian school a generation earlier—was illusory: for our information about Jesus' mind is very restricted indeed. But a truth of permanent Christian significance had none the less been rediscovered.

Our Lord is shown to us in the gospels as one who asks questions for information. He denies knowledge of the timing of the Day of the Lord (Mark 13.32). His words presuppose commonly accepted beliefs about the Old Testament. St. Luke says that Jesus "advanced in wisdom" (2.52, cf. the allusions to Christ's earthly life in Heb. 2–5). Theologians were at first very perplexed about the dogmatic implications of all this. If Christ's human experience was quite literally what the Gospels imply, how could he at the same time be said to be God the Son? Gore put forward the view that passages such as Philippians 2.5–11 permit us to think that, in becoming man, Christ "emptied himself" of the exercise of some of the divine functions. The *kenotic* theory, as this is called from the Greek word "to empty", had been elaborated in Germany in the middle of the last century, and advocated by a Scottish divine named Bruce in 1881 in a striking book called *The Humiliation of Christ*. It was advocated by scholars as different from one another as Bishop Weston of Zanzibar and Principal Forsyth. Some writers continue to use kenotic language, but generally speaking the theory has not held its ground. So extraordinary a metaphysical doctrine would require vastly more support than a dubious exegesis of Philippians 2.5–11 to be believed. Some have objected to the kenotic theory on the ground that it sounded mythological; but it is no more mythological than the views it was designed to replace. To imagine the Son temporarily handing over the control of the universe is no more fanciful than picturing him governing the stars from the manger. Ways must be found for describing God's action in Christ which avoid this kind of language altogether.

Other writers at the beginning of the century, equally diverse, suggested lines of thought not unlike the ancient Christology of Antioch. Isaac Dorner in Germany had already described the Incarnation as a progressive union of the divine Logos with the human nature of Jesus as his mind and will grew. William Temple and William Sanday suggested views not unlike this. Their efforts were not well received at the time, but they have turned out to be more fruitful than the kenotic theory.

If Christ is different *in kind* from the saints, his union

with the Godhead must have an ontological basis. In patristic times it was the idea of an ontological union that was thought to be the most difficult aspect of the Incarnation. To scholars of the nineteenth and early twentieth centuries on the other hand, the psychological aspect was the difficulty—how could a man with a limited consciousness be said to be divine? Karl Adam, who worked hard to pursuade his Roman Catholic co-religionists to take Christ's manhood in earnest, continued to believe that the ontological union was the greater mystery. We have plenty of human analogies, he says, for the penetration of one personality by another.

The recognition of our Lord's genuine manhood makes many things in the gospel story more intelligible. For example there is the matter of his works of power. Jesus is as different as could be from H. G. Wells' *Man who Worked Miracles*. He does not give the impression that his works were done by the flick of a magic wand. The power to heal is described like a physical strength leaving his body. In the abnormal powers of mind over body under great moral or religious impetus, we catch glimpses of the potentialities of human nature. Instead of being interventions of omnipotent power, our Lord's deeds mean a great deal more if they are looked upon as revealing the whole truth about man and the indwelling of spirit in matter. This view was put forward as early as 1896 by A. J. Mason, an Anglican theologian of unimpeachable orthodoxy.

It might be thought that New Testament scholarship and Christology had now wedded to give us back the Jesus who really lived, the Jesus whom men may love and worship and imitate. The work begun by St. Bernard when he rediscovered the power of affective prayer to Jesus might be thought to have reached its fruition. How deep has been

this desire to get close to the manhood of Jesus can be seen
if we look at St. Ignatius Loyola (d.1556). He conceived
a scheme of spiritual training, embodied in his *Exercises*,
the object of which is to draw into play every faculty of the
mind. Each meditation begins with a preliminary called
composition of place, which means fixing the imagination as
realistically as possible on some scene, say, in our Lord's
life. Before he founded his Society, St. Ignatius went on
pilgrimage to Palestine. On one occasion, he gave away
his pocket knife to the Turkish guard, to be allowed to have
one more look at our Lord's (supposed) footmarks on the
Mount of Olives, so that he could for ever remember
exactly how Jesus was standing the moment before his
ascension. This attitude to the incarnate life has not only
trained the Jesuits, it has struck deep into the devotional
life of the west. St. Ignatius shows what the majority of
Christians would like to be able to do with the gospel story.
But can we have our Jesus like this—and ought we to want
to?

The unique and completely real personality of Jesus is
stamped on every line of the New Testament. I Corinthians 13 does not even mention his name, yet it is a perfectly drawn likeness of the Jesus of the gospels. The gospel
is Jesus Christ himself, not his sayings, not a quality of
life derived from him: Immanuel, God coming in this
specific person, is the essence of the kerygma. The word
became flesh and tabernacled among us, says St. John: this
is the consummation of God's grace and truth. We have
seen him with our very eyes; our hands have actually
touched him, says the first epistle of John. The Fathers
looked upon the Incarnation as the key to the proper
understanding of human nature and the *raison d'être* of the
created universe. In modern times, the construction of a

philosophy that has Christ as its starting-point has taken on a new urgency. From the time of Darwin, it is becoming clearer that nothing will match up to modern knowledge short of an organic philosophy—that sees matter and evolving life as the progressive unfolding and expression of spirit and purpose and personality. Bergson, Whitehead, L. S. Thornton, Raven, Teilhard de Chardin and others have been striving towards such a philosophy. Not all have been professing or orthodox Christians, but the Incarnation has been a guiding star and will certainly go on being so. Others again have looked to the Incarnation for the basis of a satisfactory doctrine of work, of home, of human relationships in political and racial questions.

The New Testament witness to Christ's saving acts is also unequivocal. By his healing of men's souls and bodies, as well as by his words of authority, Christ proclaimed the presence of the kingdom. That his dying and rising were God's victory over evil is the reason *why* Jesus is the gospel. But it is upon the *consequences* of what Christ did that the New Testament writers rivet our attention. They only tell us about his earthly life in so far as it bears directly upon our worship and living here and now. Jesus left no letters and diaries that we can edit and weave psychological biographies around; nor have we any tit-bits from his friends. The New Testament writers lived quite close enough to our Lord's lifetime to have been able to give us this sort of thing if they had believed it to be of the slightest value. What they give us is enough and wonderfully sufficient; anything further might only pander to pious fantasy or even an adoration of the manhood of Christ for its own sake. This may all sound a little austere, but we must take biblical theology seriously in this as in other respects. It is interesting, incidentally, to look at the quandary of Christian art, now that the florid artifices of the baroque are no longer acceptable—haloes and cherubs and all. How shall Jesus be represented, they wonder; dressed like an Arab, or a workman in a cloth cap, or a young man of the sixties with long hair?

We must now return to the rough-and-tumble of New Testament criticism. In the last chapter we saw that one of the most remarkable episodes was the creation in the nineteenth century of the *liberal* picture of the life of Jesus. Jesus, it was held, both proclaimed and embodied the ideals for mankind. A life completely dependent upon God as Father, and dedicated to the brotherhood of man, had become a living reality in Jesus. The heart of it was his consciousness of sonship. Every human consciousness is unique; things happen to *me* in a different way from that in which they happen to everyone else. Indeed, each of us could almost believe that the universe is a dream in his own mind. In spite of our separate experience, however, we can speak of sharing someone else's feelings, and our private world can and does condition the quality of other people's. Jesus' awareness of being Messiah, Suffering Servant, beloved Son, was in fact the source of Christianity. It was his experience that was communicated to others. The gospel therefore carried its own verification with it. No longer did Christianity need to be propped up with tortuous arguments from miracles and the fulfilment of prophecy. If it had been rightly understood, it would never have needed these things, for it could be tested in the heart and experience of any man. For many nineteenth-century thinkers, this kind of argument was not meant to be a substitute for orthodoxy but a reinforcement of it. For Coleridge, the Bible is true because "it finds me" at every level

H

of experience. His theology of the Trinity and Incarnation were orthodox; he believed in the historic foundations of the faith, but thought that rational arguments, true though they were, had been allowed to swamp the ship of faith on its wonderful voyage of discovery. Too many people still take their views about the German liberal theologians from Schweitzer. Some of the exegetical views of these men have had to be rejected; but Schweitzer was a very poor judge of the stature of men like Schleiermacher, from whom we have a great deal to learn.

If we look closely at the structure of Ritschlian theology —the most sophisticated form of German liberalism—we find that it has two separate yet dependent elements. First, there is the fact of Jesus with his unique consciousness and message. Secondly, there is the *value judgement* which the believer puts upon the facts—and this is the act of faith. It was thought that the facts about Jesus could be sufficiently established by a purely rational process of historical study. If the layers of church dogma, Jewish mythology and legendary accretion were stripped off, Jesus could be seen as he really was. The value-judgement could then be made by looking at man's spiritual needs and the way in which Christ fulfils his highest aspirations. Faith was the capacity by which man recognised Christ as the answer to his life—a faculty analogous to that by which lovers recognise their mutual fulfilment.

There is a great deal of truth in the way that Ritschlianism described the working out of Christianity: it builds a real bridge between what happens inside our personality and what Jesus experienced and communicated. The rationalistic theology which it replaced had almost evacuated *faith* of any meaning—for according to the apologists from Tillotson to Paley, a man believed in

Christ because he was convinced by the proofs of supernatural power, like the fulfilment of prophecy and the
working of incontrovertible miracles. Ritschlianism swung
the pendulum too much the other way. Lutheran orthodoxy had always had a phobia about any tendency to make
faith dependent on *reason*, on philosophical analysis or the
evidence for biblical history. Ritschlian liberalism thought
it had discovered a way of cutting faith and reason clean
apart. But time has shown that this was not easy, and the
scheme as we have described it has had to be modified
in at least two important ways.

First, the portrait of Jesus has had to be drastically rewritten since Schweitzer. Secondly, the idea that Christian believing and historical study can be kept in separate
compartments is much too simple to be true. Let us take
these points one by one. The dreary picture Schweitzer
paints of the young broken-hearted prophet has no *ex
cathedra* claim to objectivity—for he tinkered with the
evidence as much as the academic predecessors whom he
denounces. Jesus' ethic, it is true, is quite unlike a social
programme or a body of casuistry—it is extraordinary that
anyone should ever have thought it did resemble either.
The parables, sayings and symbolic acts are a heralding of
immediate crisis. In the face of this, every commonplace
value is turned upside down: men must be prepared to
cut off their right hand or pluck out their eye, to hate
father and mother, to lose their very life, rather than forfeit the moment of grace. This is not the delusion of a man
who thought the end of the world was round the corner.
Barth, Dodd, Bultmann, and all who have read the gospels
to us in an existentialist light, have done immeasurable
service by showing that the teaching and example of Jesus
reach the very heart of truly human living. Wideawake

human life consists of decision; and Christ is the yardstick
by which all human values can be measured. His teaching
has gained—not lost—in the universality of its meaning
since the coming of biblical theology.

Our present-day picture of the ministry and death of
Christ also has a different perspective from that commonly
accepted in the nineteenth century. The earliest Christian
writings describe the Crucifixion neither as an unfortunate
interruption of an idyllic life nor as a martyrdom in a good
cause, but as the climax of a divine strategy. The evidence
that Jesus believed it to be his mission to suffer as *the*
prophet is manifold. Now unless he were a pervert,
this suffering must have had a redemptive meaning for
him. The Jesus of the "hard sayings" and the road to the
Cross is very different from the "gentle Jesus" of much
nineteenth-century piety. When Sir Edwyn Hoskyns'
commentary on the fourth gospel was published in 1940,
it was not a landmark in gospel criticism but it did open
the eyes of many people in this country to the stark realism
with which Barthians were looking at our Lord. One
bishop wrote in horror that this was not the Jesus he had
known. The nineteenth-century theologians had not been
wrong in looking for the heart of the gospel in the historical Jesus; they had simply not been prepared to take him
as he looks at us from the pages of the gospels, with his
stern demands and ruthless denunciations and uncom-
promising assertions about the supernatural activity of God
in the affairs of men.

We must now see what has become of the twofold plan
that the Ritschlians laid out to describe the activity we call
faith. It was thought that there were ascertainable historical facts on the one hand, and value-judgements on the
other. We must recognise to begin with that some of the

most crucial things which Christians believe in are either not historical statements at all, or they are assertions about the meaning of events which no ordinary historical study could possibly adjudicate. There was a funny story about a modernist bishop who was said to have analysed the creed historically, and found that all he had left was "I believe in ... Pontius Pilate". But look at a central Christian affirmation like "Christ died for our sins". That Christ died is a plain historical statement which no one would deny—unless he thought that Jesus never existed. But what does "Christ" mean? He is the God-anointed king who fulfils Old Testament expectation. But to say Jesus is all this is to *interpret* the story about him. When St. Paul says in one of his earliest letters (1 Corinthians 15.3) "Christ died for our sins according to the Scriptures", it sounds as if he is quoting an already familiar credal formula. We are being given a value-judgement of Jesus' death. Notice also that we are not just told the story of Jesus and left to make *our* value-judgement: the epistles, and the gospels too, select the facts and give them to us along with the value-judgement of the first generation of believers. The Ritschlian idea that we can sort out the history and then put our own judgement upon it is not a practicable proposition.

What, then, are we to say about "he ascended into heaven"? Is there a historical fact here in the ordinary sense at all? And what is the nature of the statement "he rose from the dead"? At this point, Christians in the twentieth century tend to diverge; and they must agree to differ: accusations of insincerity or unfaithfulness to the gospel are as unhelpful today as excommunications would be. Conservative theologians continue to maintain that the Cross and the whole of our Lord's work is only validated if he rose from the dead in the literal sense, with the empty tomb and transformation of his physical body. An unsympathetic historian would not believe the evidence; but the rationalistic alternative explanations have all been open to grave difficulties—the Jewish authorities, for instance, had everything to gain by exposing the falsity of the belief if they could have done. The stories in Matthew and Luke about the tomb are elaborations on Mark's truncated narrative, and are not as helpful as we could wish. There also seem to be two different sets of tradition about the location of the Lord's appearances. But the Resurrection, and it alone, explains the existence of the Church with its kerygma; and it is irrational to reject the Church's own explanation of itself, especially when the event makes sense of all that Jesus did.

Others have argued that, since the evidence for the Resurrection cannot be accepted by a person who is not already disposed to put his faith in Christ, it is not true that the supposed event is the *cause* or *proof* of our faith. If we believe that anyone survives death, it would surely be Jesus who would enter triumphantly into the future life. The stories about the Resurrection are best understood as a parabolic value-judgement on the quality of his life and achievement. To burden faith with a unique physical miracle is neither necessary nor desirable. The existence of the Church and the demonstrable power of Christ in men's souls are living proofs; quite different from a miracle that requires faith before it can be believed.

This latter position has led to a further question. If Christian faith can exist without the Resurrection to back it up, in what sense is faith dependent at all on the events of the New Testament? If the New Testament has created a new realm of human experience, does it matter if it now falls away like the expended rocket that has put men into outer space? This is a matter of serious concern. As long ago as 1913, Ronald Knox asked whether we had to go on waiting for an annual bulletin from Dr. Sanday telling us what we may still believe. Knox's own answer was Rome—but today even this Cave of Adullam does not look so bomb-proof.

Two centuries ago John Wesley made a very profound study of the way in which people actually come to believe in Christ. A man seldom becomes a Christian by sifting ancient documents and weighing historical probabilities. He catches the spark of faith from a member of the household of faith and this is kindled by further contact with the worshipping community. The life of the man's spirit is made possible because of the simultaneous working within him of the divine Spirit. Any Christian can test the truth of this for himself, by searching in his memory to find how he became an active worshipper—most probably it was because a friend or a group took God and Christ seriously, and the reality of what they were doing took hold of him, and he identified himself with them. If the Christian has the bent to do so, he can follow up his experience by some study of Scripture and history—and Wesley assumed that a believer would realise that sound scholarship was being pursued on behalf of the Church. This analysis is still of great importance in pastoral theology. It has an interesting analogy in scientific research. J. S. Mill in his *System of Logic* thought he was unwrapping the essence of scientific procedure and the rational laws that govern it. But Mill was not a scientist, and he did not realise how advances in knowledge come about. Sir Karl Popper and others in our day have more accurately described the process. The investigator does not begin by combing through endless masses of data to try to isolate a pair of things causally connected: he has a sudden intuition of the truth, and *then* he begins the rigorous process of inductive verification.

Wesley understood the connection between the spiritual life of a Christian today and the things that Jesus did, and he could take on any opponent in the scholarly battle over the historicity of the New Testament—as witnessed by his reply to Conyers Middleton. But once theologians had admitted that Christian faith can flourish by the immediate power of the Bible and the fellowship of believers, the importance of the gospel history was bound to keep being questioned. At least three major attempts have been made in the present century to establish Christian faith as a category of human experience in its own right. Not that the theologians themselves doubted the role that Jesus had played—but the assertions which the church makes about him are so tremendous that they must have a credential far greater than could be supplied merely by a handful of early Christian letters. Catholic modernism before the first world war, Barthianism between the wars, and Bultmann since the second world war, though very different from one another, have all been making the attempt to shift the centre of gravity for Christian certitude.

Of the three, Catholic modernism gets the least sympathy today. Its advocates were so mesmerised by radical gospel criticism that they could not forge any real links between the dogmas of the Church and the experience of the first generation of believers. Their philosophy, moreover, was a kind of immanentist idealism, out of favour today. But they did try very hard to show how the Catholic religion—as a going concern—meets man's spiritual needs; and Baron von Hügel in his person and writings is a shining example of the kind of fruits the movement might have borne if it had not been ruthlessly suppressed by Pius X.

Barthianism practically created biblical theology as we know it—the most realistic study of Scripture that Christian history has witnessed. Yet it has had this other aspect: beginning from the living power of the word in the Church today, it comes to seem almost blasphemous to think that belief in God or the authority of his word needs to be bolstered up by rational arguments or historical research. Man's first duty is to *hear* the word of God in his particular situation and *obey* it. At a time when men of other reformed traditions were worried about whether we can still believe in the Virgin Birth or the nature miracles, Barthianism seemed to speak with a fresh voice of authority—these problems seemed to matter very much less. Amazingly conservative views about the Bible began to reappear. But to others, Barth seemed to have shown that the gospel is really about something that can happen to men now.

Thus it appeared to Rudolf Bultmann. He had gone all the way with Barth in grasping the truth that the Bible is not just a voice from the past but the sacramental vehicle of God's will now, whenever it is listened to in faith. He was in addition a pioneer in the form criticism of the gospels; and understood before anyone else did that the various pieces out of which the gospels are made up are all different ways of picturing the kerygma, the central message of Christianity. But before all this, Bultmann was a pastor—he had been an army chaplain in the first world war—desperately earnest about communicating the gospel, yet appalled by the impossibility of doing this with the trappings of traditional biblical and ecclesiastical language. So he asked himself: What is the kerygma, the central truth that every scrap of the gospels is bearing witness to? It is that God's grace—his love and purpose towards us—

is manifested in Jesus Christ. Because of their latent fear, men camouflage the real human predicament with a thousand and one distractions and excuses. Jesus threw aside every pretext of safety and convention, and in proclaiming and obeying the absolute demands of the kingdom of God went to a certain death. But in that abandonment of make-believe he broke into authentic life, and he unlocked the secret of life in God's world for all men: "When thou hadst overcome the sharpness of death, thou didst open the kingdom of heaven to all believers." Here is a message, Bultmann contends, that can boldly be presented to all men without the embarrassment of antique ideas.

It goes without saying that a great many theologians reject *in part* his programme for demythologising the creed —for he not only dispenses with angels and demons, but alleges that the doctrine of the Incarnation, and the trinitarian theology that follows from it, is based upon an Iranian myth of a *heavenly man* which had seeped into Jewish circles. The inference that such a myth preceded the Christology of the New Testament is much more slender than might be supposed from the eminent names who subscribe to the theory. Be this as it may, the debate about the extent of symbolism in the creed and the New Testament is bound to go on. Bultmann is certainly right about this: if the gospel is to be commended to our humanist-minded world, we have got to show what it means and what possibilities it opens in the language of real human experience. We are obliged to go on using the language of myth, because it is there in the Bible, the liturgy and Christian history; but we must explain what it means for finding God through the human situation. A writer such as Professor John Macquarrie is engaged in this most valuable task: for he embraces the practice of the Catholic religion as an Anglican and at the same time shares Bultmann's pastoral urge to make the traditional language practically intelligible.

"How far is it to Bethlehem?" We seem to have come a long way—from ancient Alexandria and Antioch, via St. Bernard and St. Ignatius, John and Charles Wesley, Ritschlians, modernists and Barthians, down to Bultmann. Towards the end, it has looked as though some theologians have wished to jettison the Jesus of history. But this is not so—the whole story in its amazing complexity bears witness to the Christian certainty that in Jesus of Nazareth we find the key to life, the unveiling of the mystery of God.

CHAPTER SIX

The Son and the Servant

When we looked at the Old Testament in chapters 2 and 3, we saw the way in which modern scholarship has highlighted its distinctive theology. The study of the New Testament has a certain counterpart to that of the Old. For a long time, interest was concentrated upon the *differences* between the books. There was the apparent contrast between the fourth gospel and the synoptics, and above all there was the hundred-year old contention of Bauer that St. Paul's gospel was something radically different from that of the primitive Palestine Church. Today there is no lessening of interest in the fourth gospel or the synoptics or St. Paul; but there is an awareness that the things the New Testament writers have in common are infinitely more significant than their differences in presentation. Behind the outwardly varied appearance is the one proclamation of the saving acts of God in Christ. One of the landmarks in this new understanding was Dodd's book called *The Apostolic Preaching* in 1936. Just as we now have books like von Rad's and Eichrodt's *Theology of the Old Testament*, so we now have works like Richardson's *Introduction to the Theology of the New Testament* and Stauffer's *New Testament Theology*. Most Christians still treat the Old Testament merely as a preparation for the gospel, and not as a serious part of divine revelation in its own right. Hence our practical understanding of the life of the Church as a people under covenant is still impoverished. The same is true of our understanding of the New Testament. The basic truths about the mission of Christ and his body are highlighted for us by twentieth-century scholarship, but the down-to-earth consequences of this have as yet scarcely been grappled with.

The Apostolic message comes across in different forms. A letter about Church discipline by St. Paul looks quite different from the portrait of Christ given by one of the evangelists; their wording too seems to put the emphasis upon different things. A deeper comparison reveals their profound unity. St. Paul, for example, speaks about the initial wonder of the new dispensation as God *justifying* the sinner through his grace: but this is the very same thing that we read about in the gospels, when Jesus eats with publicans and sinners. To study the kerygma we must, to begin with, take Jesus' words and deliberate actions together. This is not because he practised what he preached, as one might say, but because what he did was believed by him and his disciples to be the divinely-ordained instrument for bringing in the kingdom. Then again, the words and deeds of Jesus have to be read alongside the interpretative teaching of the epistles. St. Paul's early letters were probably written years before the real teaching about Jesus was committed to writing; but their emphases should not be given priority over the gospel tradition, as has often happened in systematic theology. What follows is not meant to be a pocket guide to New Testament theology, but an enquiry into the practical priority that

we should give to a few of the themes that biblical theology
has brought to the fore.

THE SON

"Abba, Father," said Jesus in Gethsemane. Professor
Jeremias and his research team have searched the whole
mass of ancient Jewish literature, and have found not one
single instance outside the New Testament of God being
addressed as Abba. In this intimate colloquial word by
which a Jewish child might address his human father we
surely touch the real historical Jesus with his unique gift
to the experience of mankind. Here is a familiarity—
not of the kind that breeds contempt—but that springs
from unbounded reverence, love and confidence. If
Abba is Jesus' characteristic word for God, it must
underlie the passages in the Sermon on the Mount where
he speaks of the Father's uncaused love—making his sun
to shine on the just and unjust; of the Father's complete
knowledge of the motives of those who worship him; of
the Father's constant creative activity towards man, as he
feeds the birds and clothes the grass; and above all, the
Lord's Prayer must have begun "Abba, who art in
heaven . . ."

That the Almighty and All-holy can be known intim-
ately and personally is the sublimest of Christian truths—
it is also, paradoxically, the easiest to trivialise. Yet it is
the most daring assertion about the nature of man's
material and spiritual environment that could be made.
Nature is now revealed to us by science as a network of
fantastically complex contrivance. Every scrap of living
material, from the microscopic virus or plant, is built out
of cells—each programmed with built-in instructions on

how to feed, to grow and to reproduce. It is not difficult to believe in an underlying unity, a *ground* of all being. The real question now is concerned with the character of what lies at the heart of things. The old materialism with its picture of matter like random billiard balls is too naïve to trouble about. Even the mathematical odds against a situation arising in which a world of creatures could evolve and live together are colossal. Given the universe, with its mysterious unity in complexity, which tells us most about its character, the molecule or the child's love for its father and mother? Jesus' answer is categorical. Yet, it may be asked, have we not here the classic example of the creation of the fictitious father-figure? This brings us to what, without any apology, we can call the Freudian swindle. Wittgenstein was no Christian believer, but he clearly points out the topsy-turvy *non sequiturs* in Freud's reasoning. Here is a good example of this non-logic: man creates a father-figure, therefore, there can be no such thing as a universal father. But why? Numerous writers have continued to point out that logically the opposite could be the case—man's intuitive belief that a personal and good being stands behind and within nature may, to say the very least, indicate the ultimate truth. Every aspect of the life that men live in common is affected by our belief about the character of the reality in which we exist. When someone complains "It isn't fair!" he is confessing that at the heart of things he believes there is a right and wrong, which has nothing to do with men's pleasure, profit or convenience.

The fatherhood of God is also seen in the New Testament as a model for all those human relationships in which one man has some responsibility for the well-being of others. *Paternalism* is a dirty word today: this is tragic, and it must derive from a false conception of fatherhood. "This is in accord," says St. Paul, "with his (God's) age-long purpose, which he achieved in Christ Jesus our Lord. In him we have access to God with freedom, in the confidence born of trust in him . . . I kneel in prayer to the Father, from whom every family in heaven and on earth takes its name . . . " (Eph. 3.11–15 N. E. B.) The parent in the human family is to be loved and trusted and be responsible in a way analogous to God. So also the apostles viewed their fatherhood in the Christian ministry: "My son", "My children" are phrases continually on the lips of St. Paul, St. Peter and St. John. In some respects, it is more imperative today to study the diversification of responsibility in mankind than to rest simply in the truth that all men are equal.

The correlate of Abba is the word Son. "Everything is entrusted to me by my Father," says Jesus, "and no one knows the Son but the Father, and no one knows the Father but the Son and those to whom the Son may choose to reveal him" (Matt. 11.27; Luke 10.22). The wording of this synoptic (Q) passage is so reminiscent of the fourth gospel that it has been called the Johannine thunderbolt. Its authenticity has been denied by many scholars on the ground that it shows a hellenistic idea of communion with God. Jeremias claims it to be thoroughly Jewish in spirit and the rendering of an original Abba-saying of Jesus. It is indeed very close to the Old Testament prophets in their belief about being "known" by Jahveh. The passage in fact brings us very close to the heart of this central theme of the gospels—the mission of the Son. For Jesus not only speaks of the fatherhood of God and the sonship of man in universal terms, but of a unique Sonship as well. The name Son is one of the most important link words in the New Testament for describing the person and function of Jesus.

Two long traditions of Old Testament thought are fused together by the name Son—the Messiah and the prophet. The very words heard at Jesus' baptism: "Thou art my son, my beloved; on thee my favour rests" (Mark 1.11) are a conflation of Psalm 2.7 and Isaiah 42.1, the beginning of the first Servant poem. Psalm 2 is a royal psalm, addressed to a newly anointed and enthroned king of Judah. In many of the ancient civilisations, the king was actually a divine figure—literally the son of God. In the Old Testament of course this was not so; but the king was anointed in the name of Jahveh, and in a special sense he was his son. In II Samuel 7, we have the remarkable oracle spoken about the house of David by the prophet Nathan, and one should consider the almost priestly role that Solomon plays in the dedication of the temple. Modern study of the wording of some of the psalms also suggests that the king played a more important part in the annual Hebrew ritual than is apparent from the historical books. From all this grew the prophetic belief in the coming of the future scion of the house of David, the Messiah. The title Messiah, Christ, had come to have such political overtones that our Lord simply could not have overtly used it during his ministry; yet it is certain that the earliest Christian proclamation was that the crucified Jesus was Messiah. We are not concerned here with the intricacies of this question: did Jesus, for example, give a categorical affirmative to the high priest when he was challenged about his Messiahship? The point for us is that from the inception of the Church's mission at Pentecost, Jesus was proclaimed to be the victorious king. This is the primary New Testament doctrine of salvation. More often than not this has been swamped in Christian history by other doctrines about the Atonement. Gustav Aulen

I

back in 1931 in an important little book called *Christus Victor* drew attention to this fact. We use the term Christ incessantly, without realising that we are talking about a king and his kingdom. We sing "The strife is o'er, the battle won" at Easter, and seldom remember at other times that this was the first meaning given by disciples to the gospel. Further consideration of this theme must wait until we have said something about the servant-prophet.

From the revelation of God as Abba and the significance of the Son, together with the experience of the power of the Spirit, flows all the New Testament language about the Trinity. It is time that Christians became less coy about their belief in the Trinity: it is not an intellectual extravaganza but the experience of the New Testament men spelt out. The Faith was never about God *out there* or God *in here*, but something we can only describe as multidimensional. The experience of the Father, the Son and the Spirit was a life *in depth*; and we cannot understand what the writers are saying unless this is kept continually in mind. The very fact of becoming a Christian is to enter a threefold relationship with God—men are to be baptised "in the name of the Father, and of the Son and of the Holy Spirit" (Matt. 28.19). The fact that men from both Gentile and Jewish backgrounds can come to know God as Abba because they are in Christ the Son is the very hallmark of the presence of the Spirit (Gal. 4.6; Rom. 8.15). There are practical consequences drawn from the multi-relationship as we shall see later.

The names, Father, Son and Spirit, are used ontologically in the New Testament: that means, they are intended to tell us things about God's *being*—and not simply how men feel about God. It is absurd to say that living *as if* there were a heavenly Father is the same thing as living in the faith that *there is* a heavenly Father. Father, Son, Spirit are therefore a different type of word from a title like Lamb of God—which is a value-judgement on what Jesus accomplished. Both kinds of word, however, are used functionally in the New Testament: Father, Son, Spirit, Christ, Son of Man, High Priest, are meant to tell us what God was, and is, doing for us through Jesus. This is a commonplace of theology today, and can be studied in a large work like Cullmann's *Christology of the New Testament*. But prayer and practical reflection ought also to begin here. "O Lord God, Lamb of God, Son of the Father . . ." still rolls off the tongue with seldom an enquiring glance at the practical meaning of any one of the titles and words.

For the moment, let us ask what it means to know God as Abba in the context of our adopted sonship with Christ. The word which springs to mind from Jesus' teaching to express this is *faith*. The hopes and ideals of the old Israel were focused and fulfilled in Jesus; and the new Israel began to fan out from him when a group of fishermen said "yes" to his call. The sequence of two verses in Mark 1.15, 16 is most instructive. "The time has come; the kingdom of God is upon you," says Jesus as he opens a new aeon for mankind—"Jesus was walking by the shore of the sea of Galilee when he saw Simon and Andrew . . ." A contrast apparently so banal, yet this is what the kingdom is all about. Simon and Andrew could scarcely have had an inkling of what lay ahead—but their decision began the Christian church. Like ancient Israel, the Christian religion did not begin with a theory but with a call and an experience of God's love demonstrated in his power to save and remake men. There was much more to it than an exciting mission campaign with Jesus, as they found; and religion should not be narrowed into what von Hügel called "Christism". But the personal human allegiance to our Lord has still a weighty pastoral appeal. Men will water down a principle or lightly regard an institution, but personal disloyalty to our Lord is something that few will look right in the face once they have known Christianity in this way.

There is no longer any excuse for the survival of the idea that faith is (a) a purely intellectual activity or (b) a pale irrational substitute for knowledge. It is an integrated human activity and therefore it is made up of both intellectual and intuitional elements. We may know a man in that special way in which personal beings can commune, but it involves knowing *facts* about the man. The closest analogy to faith is the illumination and creative activity of friends, colleagues or lovers. Far from being a naïve, primitive attitude belonging to the childhood of our race, faith is pre-eminently adult. "Before this faith came," says St. Paul, "we were close prisoners in the custody of law . . . the law was a kind of tutor in charge of us until Christ should come . . . For through faith you are all sons of God in union with Christ Jesus" (Gal. 3.23–26 N. E. B.). Faith is not a passive state but a positive activity. Just as physical life—let alone scientific research—demands unswerving trust in the unity and consistency of nature, so faith is a stepping forward into the spiritual adventure with Christ.

What then is man, who is able to enter into such a relationship with God? Is such an activity even conceivable? There is no contemporary question and anxiety greater than that of man's self-identity. "The proper study of mankind is man" said Pope two centuries ago, but the two avenues to self-knowledge leave a more aching void between them. Biochemistry, psychology and the social sciences seek to fit man more tidily into organic nature; yet literature and the graphic arts grope restlessly round the walls of man's consciousness; and the self-destroying force of evil remains as intractable as ever. Man has a brain of ten thousand million nerve cells, each of which can perform an operation in the thousandth part of a second. But even this magic loom is not the most striking aspect of his life. He has an unquenchable certainty of his own freedom and power to initiate purposeful activity. This is not the mere ability to choose between various physical desires, like tea or coffee—it is bound up with the other experiences vital to his selfhood: his knowledge of good and evil, of beauty and ugliness; his power even to forfeit his life for the sake of another. Is it too much to believe that the key is for man to realise himself to be a son of God? Man's intellectual stature and moral enigmas cry out for a purposeful explanation. Nothing short of this is what the New Testament claims to offer. It is not a way of resolving one particular problem, man's guilt sense, but of entering the whole life which God intends. The New Testament does not say, let us pretend that all is well: the dislocation and distortion is looked right in the face. It says that a fruitful life with God can be lived even under present conditions, leading to an ultimate fulfilment, that in everything God "co-operates for good with those who love" him (Rom. 8.28). Freud, Jung and Adler fail to offer anything substantive, because they take man as he is for their norm, with his sexual greed, his self-assertiveness and his intellectual pride. Jesus calls men to become what in essence they are—sons at home in their Father's house. The epistle to the Hebrews draws a very profound lesson for Christians by contrasting Jesus, the son at home, with all the freedom and peace that this implies, with Moses, who had to justify himself as a faithful servant (Heb. 3).

Our Lord's life provides many clues to this life of a son at home. Men have often tended to think about life in contrasts: the sacred and the secular, the contemplative and the active. Could anyone make such distinctions (except on a quite superficial level) who took the gospel material as his norm? The one meaningful dichotomy for Jesus is whether men are for or against the kingdom. Everything that is for the kingdom is sacred, however bread-and-butter; everything against it is diabolical, however religiously dressed up. The contemplative and active go hand in hand for him. Day after day he pours out his human strength to the last drop—never afraid to be weary and frayed; night after night he returns to fully conscious communion with the Father, the source of ever new life. Here are the dynamics of the life of faith. Most people are afraid of exhaustion; and when they talk of peace, what they really mean is absence of demanding responsibility. "So do not be anxious about tomorrow" says Jesus: look at the rhythm of nature and imitate that. Let your life go out from the Father to the life of the world, and then let it come back to be renewed.

THE SERVANT

Jesus conceived it to be his mission to proclaim the imminent coming of the kingdom of God and to suffer as *the* prophet of the end-time. The Hebrew-Jewish belief about the end-time goes back at least as far as the eighth century B.C. Amos speaks about it as an already established belief (chap. 5). If we look at Isaiah 60 we see a

glowing picture of the Jews as the centre of a world religion
and world empire; but when this dream did not come
true with the return from exile in Babylon, the attention
of many devout Jews in the next five hundred years came
to be fixed on the future—on a supernatural deliverance,
including a resurrection of the faithful dead. The expectation of the coming of *the* prophet goes back at least as far
as Deuteronomy 18.15, where Moses is represented as
predicting another prophet *like himself*. The idea of a
second Moses—with all it implies of a second exodus and
second covenant—underlies a multitude of allusions in the
New Testament in which Jesus is compared to and contrasted with Moses. Everyone forms an interior image of
himself, which affects everything from the great decisions
of life to a man's demeanour. A man becomes absurd or
unhappy if his self-image is too big or too small for him;
but when the image fits the man and his circumstances,
his life is one of achievement like a key fitting a lock. Jesus
conformed his words and deeds to a composite picture
drawn from the prophets; but his teaching was not to be
one more day of grace but *the* Day of Jahveh. His sufferings were not to be one more martyrdom but *the*
gateway to salvation.

The most noticeable self-designation of Jesus in the
gospels is "Son of man". Some scholars deny that Jesus
ever used this expression except on the occasion described
in Mark 8.38—and there, they say, he was not speaking of
himself but of a coming heavenly figure. It would be
strange, however, if Jesus missed seeing—what his disciples
came to see—the amazing appropriateness of the title.
Etymologically the term means no more than an emphatic
way of saying "man" or "the man", but it echoes two
important figures from the Old Testament. First, there is

Ezekiel, the persecuted but undaunted prophet of the first destruction of Jerusalem. Like Jesus who wept over the fate of Jerusalem, Ezekiel felt the pain of the disaster of 587 B.C. in his own body (chap. 5). Secondly, there is the figure "like a son of man" in Daniel 7. It has been contended that Jesus could not have likened himself to this image because the son of man here is a figure of glory, not of humiliation. But if we read the whole of Daniel 7, we find it to be a vision of the people of God ground down by heathen armies, yet faithful through martyrdom, and *then* exalted to the presence of the Ancient of Days. It does indeed fit the mission of Jesus, who recapitulates in his own person the fate of the prophets and the faithful remnant, vindicated and exalted by God himself. No wonder the speeches in the Acts take this as their main theme—the suffering and the glorification of Jesus as God's breakthrough for his people.

The figure of the Suffering Servant of Deutero-Isaiah is never far from the surface in the New Testament. Once again, it has been alleged by many scholars that Jesus did not himself make use of this concept, and that a passage such as Mark 10.45 in which he speaks of his death as a ransom is a construction of the Early Church. Wonderful and deeply significant though the four Servant poems are, it does seem a pity that so often they have been treated in isolation from the rest of the prophetic tradition—and hence elevated to being a "problem". In fact, the poems distil the essence of the prophetic mission—as Isaiah 61 does in a slightly different way. When we think of our Lord's profound identification with the prophetic role, it is quite arbitrary to decree that he did not absorb the thought of four particular passages. (Is. 42.1–4, 49,1–6, 50.4–9, 52.13–53.12. There is not complete agreement about the exact limits of these poems nor about their relationship to the other Servant passages in Deutero-Isaiah.) In some passages in Deutero-Isaiah, the Servant is Israel personified, or the faithful remnant—redeemed by God and destined to bring light to the nations. In Isaiah 50, the Servant is clearly a martyr figure, and in 52.13-53.12 he is quite distinct from Israel—he not only restores the covenant, the right relationship with God, but atones for his people's sins by his own sufferings. The four accounts of the institution of the eucharist, in Mark, Matthew, Luke and Paul, all allude to restoration of the covenant and expiation as the epitome of what Christ had done.

Here, then, is the background against which Jesus' disciples—and we should say, the master himself also— saw the events behind the gospel story. To our Lord's conception of himself as *the* prophet, we should also add what has previously been said about his sonship. From the moment of their call, the disciples knew that Jesus' life was no posturing but a way pursued with absolute integrity. They saw the divine power to remake men at work in themselves and in others; and they saw the divine power in Jesus' acceptance of the Cross—the accursed death, according to the letter of the Law of Moses. Within forty-eight hours of the blackness of the Crucifixion, the disciples became certain that Jesus was alive—not like some disembodied spirit, a notion that would have con-veyed little to Jews—but with his same life-giving personality now demonstrated to be victorious over sin and death. As the months and years went by, the wonder of it grew: for the disciples found that they could reach men who had never even heard of Jesus, and the Lord could do the same mighty works in them as he had done in his incarnate life. This had been no flash in the pan but a new and permanent relationship that God had created in Christ. Every aspect of New Testament theology flows from this belief in a specific unique divine initiative summed up in the words, "God sent his own Son" (Gal. 4.4).

To portray the stupendous fact of Christ, the Old Testament is ransacked for suggestive imagery, and the clues given in the Lord's own words are pursued. Sometimes the lines of symbolism cross in strange shapes, like the phrase "The marriage of the Lamb", but always there are fresh insights. What Christ had achieved was greater in effect than the misfortune produced by the whole human race since Adam, says St. Paul in Romans 5: Christ is the second Adam. He is the victor—conquering where Adam failed. "The Lord said unto my Lord: sit thou on my right hand until I make thine enemies thy footstool" (Ps. 110.1): no other Old Testament passage is alluded to more often than this one in the New. Several ways of picturing the new order, however, must be looked at in more detail, because of the subsequent history of these ideas.

Before the days of police forces, there had to be some method of protecting the rights of individuals; and one such method in the near east was the *goel* procedure. Everyone had a male next of kin whose duty it was to act as goel, "redeemer". If a man were taken as a slave for debt, the goel's duty was to buy him free. He might have to ransom him from brigands, or avenge his murder. The last of these duties was the least satisfactory, because it led to blood-feuds; but the system must have had some advantages in a close-knit society. The prophets took the bold step of calling Jahveh "Israel's redeemer", goel. Had not God, so to speak, avenged the wrongs done to his people, and ransomed them from slavery in Egypt and Babylon? The next step was that the Servant in Deutero-Isaiah was metaphorically said to "ransom" the people by his sufferings and intercession; and so the goel idea became attached to the prophet-figure. The stage was set for Christ's liberating work to be described as a ransom-price, and for Christ himself to become known as "re-deemer" (Mark 10.45; Rom. 3.24). Liberation from the inward and outward dominion of sin, and freedom from the threat and sting of death—this was the heart of Christian experience; and the price—the cross and every inch of the way to it.

In later centuries, theologians would not leave this glorious metaphor alone to speak its message. "To whom was the ransom paid?" they asked; "The devil," they replied. "How came the devil to accept such a ransom when he escaped his clutches by rising from the dead?" "The human body of Christ was a trick to deceive the devil." The Cross, therefore, was like a baited fish-hook, said St. Gregory of Nyssa; it was like a mouse-trap, said Peter Lombard. It was not the Bible that needed de-mythologising but the theologians.

Again, the outward forms of worship in the old world centred upon the offering of animal sacrifices. It is a commonly held mistake that the primary object of sac-rifice in the Old Testament was the removal of moral guilt: in fact the Hebrews had much too serious a belief about their covenant responsibility to imagine that broken faith could be whitewashed by ritual gifts. The passover, for instance, was not a guilt-offering but a joyful thanks-giving. The real sacrifices that God required were spiritual and moral (Mic. 6.1–8). Cultic language thus comes to

be used metaphorically of human penitence and devotion
—"the sacrifice acceptable to God is a broken spirit: a
broken and contrite heart, O God, thou wilt not despise"
(Ps. 51.17). Along with ransom language, the cultic
metaphor is applied to the work of the servant-prophet
of Deutero-Isaiah: his faith, obedience and humility are
compared to a dumb animal whose blood is shed for the
people. No longer have we a priest offering something
else for someone else, but an intercessor offering himself.
Once again the word-pictures are ready for Christ and his
disciples to describe the new act of salvation: his blood is
shed for many (Mark 14.24); his death is an expiation
(Rom. 3.25). This lays bare the very heart of the gospel:
God *so* loved the world that he *gave*. God's will to save is
not just shown in theory, as it were; it is revealed because
Jesus' self-giving was actually and historically the cause
of all that Christians have experienced.

But the gospel of the sacrificing love of Christ has had
to undergo a tragic theological adventure not unlike the
ransom picture. St. Anselm, who demolished the ransom-
to-the-devil myth, created for medieval scholasticism the
theory that Christ paid an infinite debt owed to God's
divine honour on account of man's wrongful acts. Luther
carried this theory a stage further. He pictured an arrange-
ment between God the Father and the Son whereby Christ
endures the actual punishment which the Father would
have inflicted upon all men eternally in hell. Anselm's and
Luther's theories are derived from the cultic imagery of
the New Testament by the same process of faulty exegesis
as the ransom-to-the-devil theory was derived from the
redeemer metaphor. The literary study of typology
enables us to grasp the tremendous insights of biblical
language without the snare of mythological and rationalis-

ing embellishments. The objection to the *satisfaction* and *punishment* theories is not only their assumptions about the character of God, but that they conceive the essence of sin as specific offences to which penalties are attached, rather than as a broken relationship between God and his children. It is now sixty-six years since Moberly's *Atonement and Personality* cut a new way through the theological jungle; yet Anselm and Luther are still tenaciously clung to as norms by many Catholic and Protestant writers.

St. Paul has a very striking parabolic word of his own for picturing a man's experience of Christ. One imagines oneself in the dock at a great assize. It is God's assize, and one is found guilty of breaking the divine law—the sentence of death is a foregone conclusion. Yet a miracle happens: the divine judge pronounces acquittal. This is the meaning of St. Paul's word *justification*—it means acquittal. "But now," he says "quite independently of law, God's justice has been brought to light . . . it is God's way of righting wrong . . . all are justified (acquitted) by God's free grace alone" (Rom. 3.21–24 N.E.B.). The Reformers scored a direct hit against medieval theology by showing that the keyword means *declare* righteous, and not *make* righteous. But they went further than this. Lutheran and Calvinist orthodoxies treated—and still treat—justification as the absolute controlling doctrine in salvation theology. To say the least, this is hardly fair to St. Paul; because as well as his forensic metaphor, he has an abundance of realistic language about the believer's incorporation into Christ as a *new creature*.

The idea of a forensic situation to illustrate a truth of salvation remains very striking, however, and St. Paul was not the only biblical writer to use such a method. Look, for example, at the frequency with which "judgement", "witness", "advocate", "condemn" and their cognates are woven into the fourth gospel. The idea of undeserved gracious acquittal is one which Jesus himself might well have embodied in a parable. As it is, the parable of the Prodigal Son (Luke 15.11ff.) makes the identical point. The returning son does not even deserve the modest treatment he hopes for—a servile job. Yet he gets the full treatment of a beloved son. There is not the slightest hint that he will have to work his passage, or that someone else must pay a reparation. The whole point of the story is that God's forgiveness is utterly loving and free. God does not have to get his honour satisfied or accept an equivalent retribution. In a sense a price is paid—forgiving love does involve suffering. The father in the parable, if he had been a real father, would have suffered agonies, and only if his heart had gone with his son would it have been possible for him to receive him back in the way he did. Jesus' love and suffering not only show us what God is like but what God was doing.

This brings us straight to a New Testament mode of describing the work of Christ that has the most important practical consequences. It is, moreover, a doctrine expressed in words of the deepest human experience; and its meaning has never been spoiled by distortion or mythology. Speaking about the healing of a distressing situation that had almost ripped one of his little churches away from him, St. Paul says "From first to last this has been the work of God. He has reconciled us men to himself through Christ, and he has enlisted us in this service of reconciliation. What I mean is, that God was in Christ reconciling the world to himself, no longer holding men's misdeeds against them, and that he has entrusted us with the message of reconciliation. We come therefore as

Christ's ambassadors. It is as if God were appealing to you through us: in Christ's name, we implore you, be reconciled to God!" (2 Cor. 5.18–20 N.E.B.) Here we have a clear statement as to what Christ's mission in the world was really all about, and we have an instance of its practical consequences.

This is not a *tour de force*, an attempt to salvage something relevant from the New Testament—it has emerged from a clear objective study especially of the epistles. Vincent Taylor, C. H. Dodd and D. M. Baillie are three names that spring immediately to one's mind. All three have shown definitively that the reconciliation theme is the most important aspect of the kerygma when looked at on its practical side. It does not need an expert psychologist to tell us that wilfulness and bad faith create barriers between a man and God, between men themselves, and even make a man hate himself. In all three spheres, Christ was discovered to have brought atonement by his very personality and life.

With nineteen hundred years of a multi-racial church behind us, we do not realise unless it is pointed out that the overwhelming proof of Christ's reconciling power to the first disciples was the fact that Gentile and Jew could sit down at the Lord's table together. It came as a revelation from God, says St. Paul "that through the Gospel the Gentiles are joint heirs with the Jews, part of the same body, sharers together in the promise made in Christ Jesus . . . In him we have access to God with freedom, in the confidence born of trust in him" (Eph. 3.6, 12 N.E.B.).

In chapter 5, we recognised the genuinely Christian instinct that looks to the manhood of Jesus to find a centre for its loyalty, devotion and inspiration. Nineteenth-century liberal theology created a figure who embodied all the noble and gentle ideals of the age—very different from the frigid and often terrifying appearance of the Christ of ancient iconography. Schweitzer then, to many people, seemed to throw the image into complete confusion, so that we could only hear a whisper of Christ's voice. Students of biblical language then began to study *concepts*, like "Son of man", "Servant of Jahveh". To most practising Christians, all this is virtually a closed book; and if they were told what is happening in contemporary biblical study, it would probably seem no more than an arid exercise in scholarly ingenuity. But if we are to know God through Jesus, and follow him, if he is in his very person the reconciler of man to God and of man to man, we have got to be able to know something about him. If we cannot piece together the exact details of each situation in his life, as St. Ignatius Loyola wanted to do, and if we cannot make him into the humanist reformer that many modern people have sought, what are we to do?

It has been urged in the present chapter that when we put together the *concepts* and look at their underlying meaning, we see through them to an intelligible personality. If one were to write a biography today, however carefully one listed the events of the subject's life, however thoroughly one catalogued his writings and investigated their effect upon others, one would not get past the reviewer in the *Times Literary Supplement* without being called "trivial", "undefinitive", "superficial", if this was all that one did. For what makes a man interesting, let alone significant, is his mind, his motives, his aspirations, his will. In other words, what we want to know about is the *image* he has of himself, and how far he is able to actualise it in his life. Is not this exactly what the New Testament tells us about Jesus? When we examine the concepts, the titles and the idealised figures, we see the very things that he put together to create the pattern for his unique vocation. In our discussion of Christ as the Son in his Father's house and as the suffering, reconciling prophet, we have already caught a glimpse of an authentic individual person; and already we have begun to see the relevance of what he was for the life of his followers.

K

CHAPTER SEVEN

The Disciple and the Kingdom

The present-day academic study of the New Testament concentrates no small part of its energies on the words and word-pictures used to describe Christ's person and achievement. At first sight this leads only into a maze of criss-cross symbolism. But the words were what the first Christians used to clothe their value-judgements, and if we want to get to the bottom of what they believed, we have to penetrate their language. Jesus himself lived in exactly the same thought-world as his disciples; and the same avenue of investigation therefore leads to a clearer knowledge of his understanding of the Kingdom and his role in it. Form criticism has tended of late to put the emphasis upon the thought-creating activity of the Early Church, and to leave all too little room for the vision of its founder. But if, as is now admitted, the crucial interpretative work took place within the first two or three decades after the Passion—and amongst Palestinian disciples—the milieu of the disciples and their Lord is so close that to distinguish their mind from his must, in some cases, be no more than a hairsbreadth. We have seen one or two examples in the last chapter of the way in which the keywords lead to the understanding of Christ's image of himself and his mission. We must now extend this understanding into the sphere of the kingdom and its subjects. Once again, only a few signposts can be put up; but there are basic questions here that should be pursued further. What should Jesus' Sonship and prophethood mean for the Christian and the Church? What should be the mission of the household of faith in the world? What should Christians expect God to do—and not to do—for them in their lives? In chapter 5 we saw something of the way in which Christians in modern times have come round to believe that Jesus shared our experience of living on the pin-point of time during his earthly life. If this is so, it is meaningful to speak of sharing the mind of Christ, and of accepting his postulates and commitments.

The New Testament writers do not call on men to imitate Jesus in any naïve fashion—like the members of a coterie often ape the mannerisms of a popular leader. In any case, they give their readers very little fodder for doing this. Even persecution and martyrdom are not glamorised. Hard times are approached with very sober realism. Stephen's death is described in some detail because it was a historic turning-point for the church; but James Bar-Zebedee's martyrdom is passed over in a single line. There is no masochism about the Apostolic Church. On the other hand, the concepts about which we have said so much—the components out of which Jesus built his image—these are commended for imitation, *mutatis mutandis*.

An obvious instance is the word Abba and all that it implies. As we saw in the last chapter, it is not only a unique word and revelation of Jesus, it is the hallmark of a believer's possession of the Holy Spirit, according to St. Paul. The practical implications of this sonship are unbounded. Perhaps the most interesting thing to a theologian about the work of Dr. Frank Lake is the way in which he has described in realistic psychological terms the characteristics of the life of faith as opposed to that of non-faith. He has discovered a world of difference between men living in fear, insecurity and bewilderment—seeking self-justification or acceptance—and those resting in God as Father, knowing that they are loved and accepted like the child in a happy home.

Remarkable things are happening today in the sphere of corporate life. If men are sons, they are also brothers: yet some of the consequences of this age-long belief are only now being let through the portcullis of consciousness. The drive for Christian unity is one example. But it is coming to be realised that even this is not a final objective. The Church is not a caste but a body within the human family, where brotherhood has been actualised by God's grace, in order that it may be communicated to the rest of the family. Hence the new approach to Judaism and the dialogue with the other historic religions. The demand that the infirm, elderly and under-privileged should be succoured—not by erratic benevolence but as a matter of right—is another outstanding characteristic of our time. Trends such as the movement for Christian unity, friendship with the Jews, the welfare state—these are not the figments of ecclesiastical fashion or political opportunism; they are mighty movements of the Spirit. In fact the ecclesiastics and the politicians are out of breath trying to keep pace with them. Much of the social responsibility of our time is not consciously religious in its motivation—much of it is overtly humanistic and atheistic. But a Christian, believing what he does about God and his family, is bound to see the divine hand at work.

As men can know God as Abba like Jesus did in his

earthly life, so his prophetic role is not to be looked at as an isolated phenomenon but as a pattern of life into which he calls his followers. As *the* prophet of the end-time he has an unrepeatable place in the history of mankind, but in gathering together the pictures of the ideal prophet, he embodies all that the true *servant* of God should be. There is no conflict between servanthood in this sense and what was said above about sonship. The servant, the "ebed Jahveh" of Deutero-Isaiah, is not flogged and sold like a chattel; it is *because* he is more than a slave that his self-giving care for others and his sacrificial death are of such value. St. Paul often speaks of himself as a slave, *doulos*, of Christ. He only once uses this word of Christ himself. But he knew the world of difference between a slave to the law and an adopted son who, for love, works like a slave.

Consider the following three sayings—they may originally have been separate utterances of Jesus, but the sequence is most significant: "And he began to teach them that the Son of Man had to undergo great sufferings, and to be rejected by the elders . . . to be put to death, and to rise again three days afterwards . . . Then he called the people to him, as well as his disciples, and said to them, 'Anyone who wishes to be a follower of mine must leave self behind; he must take up his cross, and come with me. Whoever cares for his own safety is lost; but if a man will let himself be lost for my sake and for the Gospel, that man is safe' " (Mark 8.31, 34–35 N.E.B.).

These sayings, placed at the very hinge point in the story of the ministry, show our Lord proposing exactly the same programme for his disciples as he accepts for himself. It is a commonplace experience that men obsessed with saving themselves—their health, their money, their

face—perceptibly shrink, whilst those whose self is lost
in their care for others grow in spiritual stature. But
Jesus is not talking about the saving or losing of our body
or its vitality: he is talking about the possibility or impossibility of the soul's survival. We profess to take Jesus'
person and teaching as our norm for doctrine, devotion and
practice; but do we? If we took the pivotal words quoted
above as our starting-point, the devotional life and *raison
d'être* of the vast majority of orthodox Christians would
have to be modified. Dr. Hodgson is one of the most loyal
and fair-minded Anglican theologians of our time. In a
recent article on this very subject he writes that Jesus
did not want men "as the saying goes, to accept him as
their personal saviour . . . The following he wanted was
that of men and women whose devotion to the welfare
of God's creation was such as to swallow up all concern
about their own salvation either in this world or the next."
It does not mean that prayer, worship and the sacraments
are irrelevant: in the New Testament they are means by
which men die to themselves in order to live to God and
his kingdom. Many Christians realise that new emphases
are being pressed upon them through the realistic study
of the Bible, but they try hard to justify old ways of thought
and activity, and even invent modern-looking reasons for
them. There is today a third alternative to the old-
fashioned Catholic with his penances and the revivalist
. with his personal salvation—psychological wholeness.
The integration of the personality and healing of its sick-
nesses is proclaimed as the end-product of religion. One
wonders what psychological quietness Jesus had on the
road to Jerusalem.

The Church, like the individual, can have its eyes turned
the wrong way round. Charlotte Brontë shrewdly weighed

up the Roman Church in Brussels in *Villette*: the whole
edifice from its splendid pageantry to its sacrificial lives
had one sole object—*the Church*. But the same can be true
of the smallest village chapel. The Church should be the
one organisation on earth that does not exist for itself, but
for the lost sheep.

What Jesus demands is contained in the words "take up
his cross". His hearers knew that a cross was a thing that
men were put to death on. Loyalty must be such that a
man would forfeit his life rather than betray Christ.
According to their loyalty or disloyalty, men will be
acknowledged or disowned by the Son of Man in the
presence of God (Mark 8.38). This is not a far-fetched
demand: tens of thousands of our brethren have met the
challenge in our own lifetime. But martyrdom is not for
everyone; and Jesus' imperative has got to be translated
into life in the affluent society. The antithesis of caring for
one's own bodily and spiritual safety must be the ungrudging acceptance of responsibility. If this sounds insipid
to anyone, let this fact be a danger signal to him: let him
ask himself what responsibilities he is actually bearing in
family, profession, church and society. The possibilities of
living non-responsible lives are much greater now than in
more primitive societies; and the acceptance of burdens
is not always counted for wisdom.

The word *prophet*, even in a biblical context, generally
carries with it the picture of someone denouncing social
and religious evils, declaring imminent doom and future
salvation. But the Servant poems in Deutero-Isaiah and
the beautiful sketch of the prophet in chapter 61 tell us
far more than this. The prophet is to have infinite patience
and compassion: "A bruised reed he will not break, and
a dimly burning wick he will not quench . . . he will not

fail or be discouraged till he has established justice in the earth" (Isa. 42.3–4 R.S.V.). He is "to bring good tidings to the afflicted . . . to bind up the brokenhearted, to proclaim liberty to the captives . . . to comfort all who mourn" (Isa. 61). His ministry is not simply to a church or enclave: "It is too light a thing that you should be my servant to raise up the tribes of Jacob . . . I will give you as a light to the nations, that my salvation may reach to the end of the earth" (Isa. 49.6). When we recall that Jesus meditated on passages such as these and framed his life upon them, it is hard to see how some critics have imagined that his aspirations were nationalistic and sectarian. The prophetic programme for Jesus and his disciples is far greater than Christians have yet comprehended.

With the prophetic vision we must take the cultic language of the New Testament. The oft-quoted Psalm 110 says of the victorious king, "You are a priest for ever after the order of Melchizedek." This association of the mysterious figure of Genesis 14.18 with the Davidic scion led eventually to the sublime theology of the epistle to the Hebrews where Jesus, the suffering, tempted yet spotless intercessor, is the great high priest of mankind. The old Israel had been called a nation of priests (Exod. 19.6); and the Church of Christ is likewise "a holy priesthood, to offer up spiritual sacrifices" and "a royal priesthood" (I Pet. 2.5, 9). A priest is primarily a mediator between God and man, and although the pictures which the word used to evoke have disappeared, the concept itself is of fundamental importance.

In an old-world kingdom, all power devolved from a single person; his will was exercised through a heirarchy of minions; and conversely, no one could approach the sovereign except through the minions. It was inevitable that God's kingdom should to some extent reflect the secular model. For the Jews, the minions were the hierarchy of angels; to which Christians later added our Lady and the saints. It was perfectly natural for Christ, the supreme mediator, to be pictured as the king's son, coming down to rough it with the peasants: "though he was rich, yet for our sake he became poor" says St. Paul. In the secular state of today, however, power, as it immediately affects the citizen, is diffused through a complex of government agencies and public and private corporations. We are hardly likely to sing "Christ, be thou my ombudsman" —yet this is the only figure who remotely resembles the bygone world.

Yet mediation—or "communication" as we should say today—is one of the most fundamental human concerns. Men are separate self-conscious organisms, but their interdependence is as absolute a factor as their separateness. In the case of our procreation and sustenance this is obvious: even Robinson Crusoe had a cave full of manufactured equipment. But it is equally true of the life of the spirit. The arts and sciences, morality and social cohesion, and the personal ties of friendship and enterprise all depend upon communication. Religion in essence is communication between man and God, but it also depends to a remarkable degree upon communication between man and man. Certain sects after the Reformation and the illumination movement of the eighteenth century erroneously imagined that the man-to-man element in religion was minimal. Practically all our religious beliefs come to us from our parents and friends. Every man creates a kind of magnetic field around him for good or ill within which others live. We are all mediators: the differences between us concern what we communicate and how well we do it. The New Testament says that Jesus is the great high priest—the supreme communicator. He mediates the personality and power of God to us. His saints, martyrs, doctors and pastors transmit the faith, hope and love that flow from him. Every Christian shares this priesthood, and is challenged to share in the mediation of grace and truth.

Priesthood not only conveys the idea of God communicating with man but of man communicating with God. Again the individualist asks, how can this be? Cannot every man speak directly to God? Yet Jesus is represented as an intercessor, not only in the epistle to the Hebrews, but in the gospel story. "Simon . . . I have prayed for you," he says; "Father, forgive them . . ." The epistles are full of allusions to the intercession of the apostles and of their congregations. This is God-ward priestly mediation. If we try to analyse intercession causally, it is difficult to get a satisfying answer: do our prayers change God's mind? But prayer is an act of the human will deliberately focused upon God—in this case for the sake of others. It is a corollary of belief in the Holy Spirit that God does take up and use for good every act of will that we make.

The office of the pagan and even the Jewish priest was primarily to offer up gifts on behalf of other people. Christ, like the servant-prophet figure, offered himself— his absolute obedience and love. This was both a means and an end in itself. Jesus' life and death were in very truth the cause of every blessing that Christians have or can enjoy. It was the supreme act of intercession. It was also an end in itself: for Jesus, like every man, owed perfect love and service to the Father. Each person united to Christ shares in his twofold work as priest and sacrifice; and like Christ also, his self-giving has the same double aspect—it

is for the sake of others, and it is the expression of his love
for God. "I implore you," says St. Paul "by God's mercy
to offer your very selves to him: a living sacrifice, dedicated
and fit for his acceptance, the worship offered by mind and
heart" (Rom. 12.1 N.E.B.).

The revolution in our political and social ways, therefore,
though it has altered our imagery, has not diminished the
meaning of the mediatorial and cultic language: communication and self-giving are the basic conditions for the
life and growth of the human soul. The same is true of the
kingdom of God, an outworn metaphor on the surface,
but integral to the whole Bible. Indeed, the interpreting
of this concept should be given top priority in Christian
preaching if we take the gospels as our standard—for the
. most cursory reading of them shows that the kingdom is
overwhelmingly the dominant theme.

The kingdom, "malkuth", of God means his sovereignty.
It cannot be squared with any secular utopianism however
noble, because it is not something which man makes or
upholds. God, who has made man, calls him to surrender
himself in love—"This is the first and great command-
ment." All men are *de jure* within God's sovereign realm
but its consummation belongs to the end-time. The kingdom is described in eschatological language, not only
because it has to do with the final drama of the world's
history, but because its demands upon men here and now
are unconditional. It is God's perfect gift and opportunity.
To come face to face with it is the moment of truth, because man's reaction to it is the parting of the ways.
"Children, it is the last hour" says the writer of the first
epistle of John; and the parables, as we saw, are full of the
note of impending judgement.

But it is now 1968. Jesus' ministry did not turn out to

be the immediate prelude to the ending of the world order. Therefore, whether we like it or not, we have to translate the doctrine of the kingdom into different terms from those understood by the New Testament writers. We have to turn the eschatological language about the last hour into spiritual absolutes that are true for everyone at every moment of his conscious life. Dodd's reappraisal of the gospel material helps us here: for if Jesus was primarily challenging men to faith and obedience there and then, we have living situations in the gospel story to take as our models. This does not water down the teaching about the kingdom and the imperatives of the Sermon on the Mount: it is saying transcendental things about *this* Thursday afternoon. It is as though we were now standing by Galilee or were in Gethsemane or the upper room. The emphasis in the gospels is not on how your sins can be forgiven—sin creates a barrier that must first be breached by God's grace: the major question is how God's name is to be hallowed, and his Kingdom come and his will be done here on earth. This is the first petition of the Lord's Prayer, and it ought to be the activating motive of all Christian prayer and effort. Jesus the prophet, who of course cannot perish outside Jerusalem—as he ironically puts it—is the kingdom of God incarnated, actualised. Through him, God's will is perfectly done—and it is done under the very same conditions under which his disciples must serve God. The kingdom of God does not lift men out of this world on a magic carpet: we have both to hear God speak and obey him through the medium of our material circumstances and our communication with other men. The chairs and the telephone are like a stage set that God has put us into; and the people round us are acting out their own drama and at the same time making up a play in which we have to work out our salvation. The difficulty, however, is not living with this strange sign language, but hearing and obeying God in a world in which men are partially dislocated from God the producer and from one another by their wilfulness.

The Kingdom of God is not identified with any external realm, even in the sense of an organisation, but the Church is far more than an aggregate of individual believers associated for mutual encouragement. The past century has seen a profound change coming about in the Church's understanding of itself. This has had extraordinary repercussions as we shall see. The origins of the new self-awareness of the Church go back far beyond the emergence of academic biblical theology; but the change and its repercussions represent a movement back to biblical realities. Biblical theology has come along later to reinforce what had already begun.

When Keble preached his Assize Sermon in 1833, warning men against the church's apostasy, he was not tilting at windmills. The churches of Europe, Catholic and Protestant, were widely believed to be nothing more than organs of society, if not of the state—man-made institutions for educational and philanthropic purposes. Even the devout believer tended to look at religion in individualistic terms, with church or chapel as a fitting expression of his faith. When the New Testament concepts of the *Body of Christ*, the *Bride of Christ* and the *Israel of God* are studied seriously, and the church is seen as the divinely created instrument of salvation, it is hard to understand how the shallow rationalistic ideas prevailed for so long. So much has been written about this in recent decades that further emphasis here is unnecessary.

With the decline in attendance at church services, there

is an increasing temptation to emphasise social and re-creational amenities in parochial life; but unless meaningful worship of God is fostered through the mysteries of salvation, nothing but the mere name of Christianity can survive. In fact, the deepened theological understanding of the Church has produced some remarkable effects. Just one year before Keble's Assize Sermon, the abbey of Solêsmes was refounded, and with it came the beginnings of the liturgical movement in the Roman Church. Like the rebirth of the doctrine of the Church, this revival long ante-dates academic biblical theology, but it is fundamentally biblical in character. The use of the Bible in liturgy, the biblical control of the liturgical year, the Old and New Testament understanding of the nature of corporate worship, the New Testament teaching about baptism and the eucharist—all these are now matters of constructive debate throughout Christendom.

One remarkable change will illustrate what is happening. From apostolic days, the centre of worship throughout the church was the eucharist, celebrated every Sunday with a rich ministry of the word and general communion of the congregation. When the pagan lands of the north were evangelised during the dark ages, only Easter communion was insisted upon; and non-communicating attendance at the eucharist later spread to southern Europe. The gallant attempt by some of the leaders of the Reformation to bring back full lay participation in the Lord's service only ended in the service itself being banished except at festivals. The nineteenth century saw the steady spread of regular Sunday—and even weekday—lay communion within the Roman and Anglican churches. The present century has seen the gradual spread of this practice into other reformed churches. Antiquarian studies of liturgy could not have produced such a profound development. Coupled with the deeper understanding of the supernatural life of the Church itself, this is surely a stirring of the Holy Spirit, bringing men back to what was the centre of worship and fellowship for the Apostolic Church.

When men began to be more aware of what the Church is, they began to be appalled at its disunity. The movement towards Christian unity in our time is a direct product of the reawakened biblical understanding of the Church. When the Church was thought of merely as a collection of venerable yet convenient organisations for worship and philanthropy, there was no scandal in disunity. Today it is not possible to be a Christian without praying and working for unity—not to create something which does not already exist invisibly, but to actualise in visible worship and service our oneness in Christ's body.

There is a great object-lesson here. Some people continually urge us to abandon our belief in the transcendental, the supernatural, as a factor in our thought and action. Yet the revolution in the Church's way of looking at itself has come about because Christians believe the unseen spiritual body of Christ to be more substantial and significant than its fragmented outward appearance. Men worked to make the eucharist the effective focus of worship because they believed that Christ is as truly present in it as he was when he prayed with his disciples as their great high priest in the upper room. Men do not seek Christian unity for efficiency or power or show, like a tycoon building a commercial empire, but because the one new Israel which Christ created is there already. This belief in the *givenness* and substantiality of God's kingdom is the very heart of Jesus' teaching in the gospels. As we saw in chapter 4, present-day study highlights the two sides of this teaching—the kingdom is both a present reality and yet looks to a future consummation. It is this that gives the special quality to all Christian prayer and endeavour. The Church does not delude itself with a utopian idealism in the present and the dream of a golden age in the future: it rests upon the present power of God through Christ and trusts in the faithfulness of his promises.

CHAPTER EIGHT

But for the Grace of God

All through this book, biblical and non-biblical words have been used which imply that God actually does certain things in the lives of those who belong to his kingdom. Theological analysis shows that God's gracious activity is the central theme both of the Old Testament and the New. Here must stand the real watershed between secularised, God-is-dead morality and supernatural religion. The Bible is not concerned with belief in a being who can be made use of by men in a quasi-magical way, and who snatches us out of life's battles when they get too hot for us. It is concerned with him who speaks to us through events in nature and history, calling and challenging us, ever opening up new creative situations for us, and supporting us however deeply we fall in tragedy or sin.

But what kind of help does God give? How does it affect the way in which a Christian sets about living his life? One might have thought that this was a subject of high priority; but pastors have been daunted by the weight of old theological controversies, and have been content to leave the whole matter to the experts. Western Christendom since the sixteenth century has been bedevilled by controversies about grace and free will. Even

L

the apparently monolithic Roman Church had the Jansenist controversy; while the evangelical revival was distraught with the dispute between Calvinists and Arminians. The clergy have been only too glad to leave the whole thing behind the theological college door.

But neglect has bred ineptitude in the teaching of how the Christian life works: moral issues have tended to be discussed apart from the devotional life; whilst spiritual exercise has been treated as a prerequisite of the pious. Popular exposition has tended to take two forms. On the one hand, there is a king of Pelagianism, with God's help implored at life's crises. "I've tried to be good 'cause I know that I should—That's my prayer at the end of the day" as Gracie used to sing. This is not irreligious— it is just not specifically Christian. On the other hand, we often hear God's help described in the language of vitamins and nutrients. Vitamins are not magical, but the simile they imply for religion is definitely magical and sub-Christian.

Granted, the relevant doctrines are not simple. In the last analysis, the truth about what God does has to be stated as a paradox. This is not because the subject is woolly or inconsequential, but because the end which God wills can only be achieved in a subtle way. What is this end? The Bible takes it to be the perfecting of the relationship between men and God. From the covenants of the Old Testament to the marriage of Christ and his Church at the end of the Book of Revelation, this is the theme. From the moment that living creatures had the tiniest spark of conation and could initiate purposeful action, the path had been taken that led to "the glorious liberty of the sons of God." Man's subjugation of nature, his capacity to express aesthetic, moral and religious

intuitions in the arts, his ability to enter into personal
relationships of every degree and to live heroically—all
these have been by-products and signposts to the future.
At the same time, evil has woven its triple chain of heredity,
environment and habit. Belief in an ancient golden age
may have disappeared; but gone too is the myth that evil
can be dissipated by higher material standards. The
perverseness that can embitter two individuals who once
loved each other is as mysterious and terrible as the
forces that divide nations and races.

The Bible says that the kingdom is God's gift and
creation—because he alone could initiate a break-through
into the human predicament. Such a break-through would
have to be in essence as decisive as was the original appearance of self-determining creatures. But how could it
come about? If God wants sons who can freely trust and
love him, sheer compulsion is out of the question. If man
were to become an automaton, the very process of evolution would be put into reverse. The very thing that makes
a human being is his awareness of responsibility for what
he does. We have to assume a spark of true humanity even
in the sickly child of reprobate parents—or our social
work would be meaningless. It is our selfhood that is to
grow and flower.

"I drew them with cords of a man, with bands of love,"
says God through Hosea (11.4). The contrast is between
the ropes with which one pulls an animal along and the
attraction of love which God uses. Every man's life is
gripped by a mesh of compulsions, derived from his
physical limitations and his social environment; but if a
man comes to know that his being is but touched by God's
love, this is enough to transform the whole situation. There
are plenty of human examples and analogies for the inter-

penetration of one personality by another. Some men's influence seems to obliterate the personalities they influence; others seem to be able to intensify the selfhood of those near to them. God's touch fully awakens the beings he himself has created—as the amazing variety of the personalities of his saints proves. Yet always there is a paradox, when God's influence is seen from the subject's own point of view, he is fully aware of his own choices and the persevering will-power that he feels called upon to exercise—yet he becomes more and more aware that nothing of this could happen without God within him. In St. Paul's letters we see an individual human mind and tireless relentless will; he is not even shy of talking about his physical and apostolic achievements; yet from inside, it looked like this: "I have been crucified with Christ: the life I now live is not my life, but the life which Christ lives in me; and my present bodily life is lived by faith in the Son of God, who loved me and sacrificed himself for me" (Gal. 2.20 N.E.B.).

The re-creating influence of God is described in three chief ways in the New Testament. First, there is the grace of God; secondly, union with Christ; and thirdly, the indwelling of the Spirit. Thus God draws men into a multi-dimensional relationship with himself. The characteristics of the new life tend to polarise around the Father, the Son and the Spirit—though not in an exclusive way. Often, the characteristics and the persons seem quite interchangeable, especially in the epistles. But this does not mean that the three ranges of ideas were synonymous: rather, the writers were trying to express the depth and richness of the new experience. God is neither "up there" or "in here"; but neither is he a nebulous undifferentiated influence.

The Greek word *charis*, grace, had already been used

to a limited extent in the Septuagint to represent God's loving kindness or mercy. In the New Testament it becomes a shorthand word of supreme importance. It primarily means God's attitude towards us—his invincible love and will to save. But the saving power is demonstrated in Jesus Christ; so *grace* comes to stand for everything that he was and achieved. In Christ God displays "how immense are the resources of his grace" (Eph. 2.7). Whereas sin multiplied, "grace immeasurably exceeded it, in order that, as sin established its reign by way of death, so God's grace might establish its reign in righteousness, and issue in eternal life" (Rom. 5.20–21 N.E.B.).

In this complex symbolism, God's love for man is thought of as an immense power, overcoming the cumulative destructiveness of sin. This may seem a far cry from Jesus' eating with publicans and sinners, but it is not. Healing the souls and bodies of men and women who knew themselves to be sinners; sharing the sacred intimacy of the Jewish family meal with reprobates: these were the *signs of the kingdom*—the demonstration that the divine breakthrough was taking place. For St. Paul the *sign* was rather different but equally convincing. By any decent standards he had been a good man, honestly striving to live up to a perfectionist ethic. All the time he had found himself up against an intractable wilfulness deep in his nature. To walk as a free man in God's grace, rather than to lie a condemned prisoner under the Law, is therefore a theme which continually appears in his writings.

That God loves us may be the most important single doctrine in the Bible, but it cannot today be treated as a truism. The modern pagan, like his ancient counterpart, frankly does not believe it: he believes in sheer fate, in luck. Furthermore, the Church does unimaginable harm

by teaching children about the love of God in a sentiment-
al, unrealistic way. As soon as they find out that life is
not like the Sunday school dream world, the Loving
Shepherd is banished with a sad smile as easily as Father
Christmas. But the men of the New Testament lived no
feather-bed existence: they suffered untold hardships and
persecution, and above all, they had seen Jesus done to
death. Yet these were the very men who came to the world
with the message that "God is love". We do them a grave
injustice to treat the climax of their faith as a platitude.
The very passage in which the words "God is love" occur
gives the reason why they believed it. "God is love," says
the writer of 1 John 4.9, "and his love was disclosed to us
in this, that he sent his only Son into the world to bring us
life."

But because God gives all we need, this does not mean
that the new life is easily accepted by everybody. The
barriers are on man's side. Christians wrongly torture
themselves with thoughts such as, if only the Church were
more alive all men would become believers. For the man
who will not let himself be loved or accept dependence;
for the man who will not be commanded to love, but only
do it when it suits his pride; for the hard-bitten man,
either through despair or recrimination—for these people,
religious language runs like water off a duck's back. Yet
love is the only power known to man that can open these
doors. This is not a theological figment but a fact, whether
worked by God directly upon the soul or mediated
through human love.

In some Pauline passages, *charis* can be rendered by
gift, favour, privilege or *generosity* and the N.E.B. does this.
Yet God does not simply wish us well; his will and deed are
one. So St. Paul, consciously or unconsciously, moves some

way towards equating God's grace with the new life he puts within us. In the well-known verse "My grace is all you need; power comes to its full strength in weakness" (2 Cor. 12.9), he comes back to the dynamic motif of Romans 5, the reign of grace.

In later Latin theology, the concept of grace came to take over most of what, in the New Testament, is ascribed to the work of the Holy Spirit. It can be argued that the place of the Holy Spirit was not lost sight of in the theology of grace—for the Spirit was the agent of grace. But there was a definite change of emphasis—and not for the better —for grace came to be thought of in quasi-quantitative terms. The teaching about being in (or out of) a state of grace is very close to New Testament thinking. St. Paul says to the wayward Galatians, "You have fallen out of the domain of God's grace" (Gal. 5.4). The Prayer Book thanks God for "the means of grace" and prays for an "increase of grace". This is perfectly legitimate language provided it is understood in the whole context of God's re-creating love. The *means*, such as the sacraments, have to be seen as specially significant episodes in the whole life of the believer's communion with God.

The second dimension of God's relationship with men is union with Christ. The gospels do not tell us what Jesus and his disciples did simply as pictures from the past; they are speaking of the relation of believers with the Church's Lord *now*. "Follow me", "Rise and walk", "Your sins are forgiven"—these are heard as utterances of the *living* Lord. There is nothing idiosyncratic about St. Paul's oft-repeated "in Christ"; Christians in a real, not just meta-phorical, sense are joined to Christ's being, and therefore in a sense share his incarnate experiences—whilst he in turn lives through their lives. There is nothing cosy about this Christian mysticism—as though he underwent all the grim things, and we just sing heart-warming hymns about surveying the wondrous Cross. The Church is the body of Christ (1 Cor. 12.12; Eph. 1.22; Col. 1.18), and Christians feed on Christ's eucharistic body (1 Cor. 10.16, 11.17ff.), but that body was nailed to the Cross, and union with him means sharing his self-oblation.

Indeed, "By baptism we were buried with him, and lay dead, in order that, as Christ was raised from the dead in the splendour of the Father, so also we might set our feet upon the new path of life" (Rom. 6.4 N.E.B.). Wherever we go," says St. Paul, "we carry death with us in our body, the death Jesus died, that in this body also life may reveal itself" (2 Cor. 4.10 N.E.B.). All this is done in order that man may grow to his full stature, the stature of Christ himself (Eph. 4.13). A man in Christ is nothing less than a new creation of God (2 Cor. 5.17). "For it is in Christ that the complete being of the Godhead dwells embodied, and in him you have been brought to completion" (Col. 2.9–10 N.E.B.).

The third dimension is, of course, the Holy Spirit. Behind the New Testament lies the long story of belief in the Spirit, *ruach* of Jahveh in the Old. This came especially to be associated with the prophet figure (Isa. 42.1; 61.1); but in Joel 2.28ff. a time is proclaimed when Jahveh will pour out his *ruach* upon all men.

The Spirit provides the impetus both at the outset of Jesus' ministry (Mark 1.10, 12), and that of the Church (Acts 2.1ff.). So vividly is the Spirit's guidance felt in the Church's early years that Acts has sometimes been called "The Gospel of the Holy Spirit".

The Davidic scion of Isaiah 11.1ff. is endowed by the *ruach* of Jahveh with specific gifts for mind and will; and every Christian excellence—from miracle working to administrative acumen—is looked upon as a specific gift of the Spirit (Rom. 15.19; 1 Cor. 2.4, 12.4ff.; Gal. 3.1ff.; Heb. 2.4). But there is more than this: the Spirit is thought to indwell the soul and impress a permanent character upon it. Taking up the metaphor of Jeremiah's prophecy of the new covenant (Jer. 31.31ff.), St. Paul speaks of the Spirit *writing* on our hearts; we are also *sealed* with the Spirit (2 Cor. 3.3; Eph. 13, 4.30). A Christian is a *temple* of the Spirit (1 Cor. 6.19); and the possession of the Spirit is a *first instalment* of future glory (2 Cor. 5.5). "God's love has flooded our inmost heart through the Holy Spirit he has given us" (Rom. 5.5). Under another name, all this came to be known as habitual and infused, grace.

As the Spirit moved upon the waters in the creation story, so now the Spirit plays a significant part in the final stages of the cosmic drama. We cannot but close with what is surely one of the finest passages in the New English Bible, from Romans 8.

"For I reckon that the sufferings we now endure bear no comparison with the splendour, as yet unrevealed, which is in store for us. For the created universe waits with eager expectation for God's sons to be revealed . . . Up to the present, we know, the whole created universe groans in all its parts as if in the pangs of childbirth. Not only so, but even we, to whom the Spirit is given as firstfruits of the harvest to come, are groaning inwardly while we wait for God to make us his sons and set our whole body free . . . We do not even know how we ought to pray, but through our inarticulate groans the Spirit himself is pleading for us, and God who searches our inmost being knows what the Spirit means, because he pleads for God's own people in God's own way and in everything, as we know, he

co-operates for good with those who love God and are
called according to his purpose."

Along with these remarkable passages about the grace
of God, the body of Christ and the indwelling Spirit, we
should put first the *hard sayings* of Jesus. If we take form
criticism seriously in their case, we must suppose that the
Apostolic Church looked upon these words as the measure
of God's demands upon the human will here and now.

"The gate is wide that leads to perdition," says Jesus,
"there is plenty of room on the road and many go that
way; but the gate that leads to life is small and the road is
narrow, and those who find it are few." Much of Bunyan's
imagery, derived from popular medieval religion, is much
closer to the realities of the Christian life in the New
Testament than the Calvinistic theology which he inter-
sperses in his story.

St. Paul's words match his life of unremitting toil—he
is not seeking to win God's favour but to match God's
grace with the response it challenges. Unlike the modern
salvationist, he will not even presume that he is bound for
heaven: "I bruise my own body and make it know its
master, for fear that after preaching to others I should find
myself rejected" (1 Cor.9.27 N.E.B.). Very significantly
he says, "You must work out your own salvation in fear
and trembling; for it is God who works in you, inspiring
both the will and the deed, for his own chosen purpose"
(Phil. 2.13 N.E.B.). The presence of God's re-creating
work does not lessen the human stature nor the demands
made upon man—it heightens the responsibility in pro-
portion to man's awakening to God's gift.

How then do the old controversies about faith and works
stand today? To begin with, there is an abiding profound
difference between self-justification and authentic faith.

The psychological difference is great; and biblical theology has shed much light upon the nature of faith as an activity of the whole man. In another sense, it is still as ridiculous to talk about "faith without works" as the epistle of James said it was. The human personality in the raw is not, it is true, a unitary whole: its senses, ambitions and fears tend to pull it apart. But if the saving action of God is designed to make it whole, then its response ought to be more and more that of a mind, will and life focused on a single pattern of objectives. We hear today about someone being a *dedicated* cricketer or a *dedicated* scientist—this good old Christian word has been revived, and we can use it again without any sanctimonious associations. For inward integrity, outward consistency and purposefulness and ungrudging self-giving can alone make an effective life.

CHAPTER NINE

Miracles

Three centuries after the scientific revolution, the question of miracles will not lie down. For men instinctively recognise that what is at issue is not simply the truth of this or that in the Bible but the character of our universe: What is God like? How does he disclose himself? How may he be expected to act in our lives? Indeed it only makes sense of the question of miracles to discuss it in this wider context. All too often the question has been treated as a philosophical parlour game.

In his inimitable way William Temple described a widespread assumption of his day: "that God never does anything in particular in any other sense than that in which he does everything in general." This is a fair description of the outlook of a great many professing Christians. Belief in the supernatural intervention of God was attacked by deists in the seventeenth and eighteenth centuries, and immanentist philosophies of the nineteenth located all spiritual impulses within nature and man. Today belief in the transcendent and belief in a personal God are being attacked in a variety of semi-popular books and articles. One cannot discover any notable arguments in this literature which have not been voiced repeatedly since the seventeenth century. The protest, that man is responsible to no one but himself, is made with a peculiar vehemence. One is reminded of children playing at house whilst their parents are out. They tell each other—and even callers at the door—that they own the house, whilst inwardly they know it is not true. None of the mysteries of man's situation is made one jot more comprehensible by the denial of God.

But if we do accept belief in a personal God, to what are we committing ourselves? Newman said that we ought not to be surprised at anything we find in the Bible or the history of the Church—imagine a child's surprise, he said, on first being taken to a menagerie. But this is precisely the notion of revealed religion that modern people (rightly) object to. When we look at the fabulous complexity of nature as science reveals it to us, can we honestly think of its creator tinkering about with its processes and producing bizarre phenomena just to make his presence felt? The menagerie notion of revelation is equally open to theological objection. How can we recognise the handwriting of God in revelation if it is not in character with what we know of him through the rest of our human experience? Many modern biblicists persistently refuse to face up to this question. They tell us that God revealed himself in particular combinations of events in history, but they do not show us how those events are to be sorted out and recognised. The medieval theologians—followed by the majority of representative Anglicans from Hooker and Butler to Temple and Tennant—argued that we get our basic ideas about the universe and its creator from looking at nature and our own spiritual faculties. This accounts for the presence of rudimentary religious beliefs in all civilisations. But the leading continental Protestant orthodoxies make a point of denying the reality of *natural religion*—any genuine knowledge about God apart from what the believer discerns through the Bible. It is as though they blotted out all the background on a photograph, obliterating the things that would help one to recognise the central figures and what they are doing. Barth himself talks about an *analogy of faith*, which does go some way back towards the Catholic philosophy of the *analogy of being*. Bultmann, however, pushes in the other direction. He tries to detach faith from what happened in history. He alleges that Jesus' person and life are not in themselves a revelation of God. God only reveals himself at the moment when a believer looks at the story of Jesus with the eyes of faith.

But his is not what the men of the Old and New Testaments say of their experiences. Their faith was rooted in things that happened in the real live world of cabbages and kings. So we cannot escape from looking at the Bible and asking what happened and what it meant. The men of the Bible were convinced that they actually saw God at work: can we see what they saw? We have to face the question of miracles.

Many pastors are afraid of discussing this subject with their people in the mistaken fear of undermining their faith. In fact the majority of people today are so confused that they wonder whether they can believe anything in the Bible at all. Any positive help is therefore better than none.

Like the other topics we have touched upon, the Christian belief in miracles is involved with a long history of theological debate; and it is necessary to say something about this because many people's ideas are still coloured by the outlook of previous centuries. In the middle ages, Christian apologetic was largely based upon the Church's

unbroken witness from New Testament times, coupled
with the belief in the continuance of supernatural gifts
especially to the saints. But with the break-up of unity in
the west, new theological structures had to be erected.
Protestant theologians had to work out an argument for
the truth of Christianity that would stand up to the claims
of Rome on the one hand and the erosion of rationalism
on the other. In the twin argument from prophecy and
miracles, they thought that they had a proof of revelation
which was not only logical but contained within Scripture
itself. The two best known statements of the position are
Butler's *Analogy of Religion*, 1736, and Paley's *Evidences of
Christianity*, 1794.

The New Testament alludes to many instances of the
fulfilment of Old Testament prophecy, and the Fathers
claimed this to be an irrefutable sign of divine planning.
This was an argument ready to hand for the post-Reforma-
tion apologists. Christ does indeed fulfil the Old Testament
in an astonishing way, but biblical criticism has made
many of the alleged fulfilments look very unconvincing
when taken literally.

The proof from miracles at first sight also looks
thoroughly scriptural: Moses worked miracles as tokens of
his mission, and the apostolic writers appeal to the
Resurrection as the pledge of Christ's authority and victory. According to the *evidentialist* theologians—as those
who staked everything on the argument from prophecy
and miracles are often called—a miracle was an event
beyond the power of man or the laws of nature to have
produced. It is therefore *ipso facto* a sign of supernatural
intervention. Demons are said by the Bible to be capable
of working miracles; but God-given ones are distinguish-
able by their beneficent character and by the rationality

and sublimity of the doctrines to which they testify.

This thesis involves the negative assertion that all alleged heathen miracles are either fakes or unusual natural phenomena. A special problem was raised by the history of the Church itself, in which miracles are said to have gone on happening after apostolic times right down to contemporary wonders in the Roman Church. To admit the truth of miracles in later ages would be tantamount to acknowledging the claims of the Roman Church to continuous divine authority. The Protestant apologists argued, therefore, that after the time when the New Testament canon was fixed and the church firmly established, miracles ceased to occur.

This argumentation sounds remote, but there was a time when it seemed a very vital concern. In the eighteenth century the historians Edward Gibbon and Conyers Middleton both temporarily became Roman Catholics, because as serious scholars they could not accept an arbitrary line between the miracles of apostolic and later times. The Fathers had to be believed when they testified to the history of Christianity *before* their time, but disbelieved when they spoke of miracles in their own world. Subsequently, both Gibbon and Middleton lost their belief in miracles altogether, and wrote influential critiques of early Christian history. Newman as an Anglican wrote an essay drawing the customary distinction between miracles of the Bible and alleged miracles of the Church, but on the eve of his conversion to Rome, he wrote a further essay in which he un-said his previous line, and tendentiously extolled the credibility of some later ecclesiastical miracles. All this shows what pitfalls there were in what at first sight looked like a very straightforward case for the gospel. One strange thing is that many intelligent unbelievers right down to our own day have been taken in by the either/or of the evidentialists—and believe that physical miracles are the only way in which God could convincingly communicate with men.

Before we look further at the question of revelation, we must glance at the scientific and historical issues that are raised by the evidentialist theology. Miracles were defined as events lying beyond the laws of nature: but what are the laws of nature? *Law* in this sense, if not a theological, is at least a sociological metaphor. We are really talking about the *uniformities* of nature—and Hume drove home this point. Mill thought that the work of science was to sift the superficial coincidences in order to discover nature's fundamental, ubiquitous uniformities. Hume, Mill and all like-minded thinkers were convinced that miracles do not happen: the whole edifice of science is built upon the assumption that nature does have fundamental uniformities. If a seeming miracle did turn up, science might have to broaden some statement in order to take account of the fresh data.

Theologians gradually became very embarrassed by all this. One attempt to make miracles seem more rational was to say that they were brought about in accordance with "higher laws" than those we normally observe. Early in the last century, an engineering genius named Babbage built what (if he had had electronic gear) would have been a very fine computer. He thought that it would have been a simple matter for God so to have contrived the universe that miracles occurred at particular foreseen human crises.

But scientific theory has moved far beyond Mill's picture of it. Men of science frankly confess that they are simply constructing *models* which enable them to handle

M

what we know as mass and energy. More than one model may be used to describe the same process in order to achieve different ends. A dialogue between religion and science today has to take a very different form from that which it took in the eighteenth and nineteenth centuries. The scientific assumptions on which the evidentialist theology was based have been irrevocably torn up by the roots. This does not mean that God cannot any longer be thought of as personally active in the affairs of men. Professor H. H. Farmer in his notable *The World and God* has suggested fresh ways in which we can picture God's activity, not only in the Bible history, but in our own lives.

We saw in chapter 4 how modern historiography began by separating out probable fact from legend in ancient books. This does not mean the end of the Bible's authority as many Christians go on fearing. No scholar throws the ancient authors of Greece and Rome into the dustbin be- cause they contain a number of odd legends—on the con- trary, modern techniques have enhanced their authority in some respects. When we look at the Old Testament, it is clear that a number of episodes in the tradition would require vastly greater authentication to be generally acceptable. It is not credible that God stopped the earth turning round one afternoon for the sake of Joshua's battle, nor that on another afternoon he made it turn a little in the opposite direction in order to convince Hezekiah that he would recover from his illness. The book of Jonah is a devastating satire on Israel's failure to fulfil its divine calling—not a literal story. The book of Daniel is an exciting contemporary record of the underground resistance movement around 164 B.C. when Jews were fighting for their very existence. It was not intended to be a history of the Babylonian captivity four hundred years

earlier. Some of the Elijah and Elisha stories are examples
of folklore known the world over. Far more remarkable,
however, is the fact that many of the most important
figures in the Old Testament have no miracle stories told
about them in the old sense of the word—Samuel, David,
Solomon, Jeremiah, Ezekiel, Ezra, Nehemiah. This leaves
the cycle of events surrounding the Exodus, Sinai and
desert trek. It has long been realised that all these can be
accounted for as idealised memories of providential
natural occurrences. This in no way lessens the significance
of the story of the people of God.

If the biblical miracles were not there to provide an
independent proof of revelation, why were they in the
tradition? It so happened that when the question began
to arise in this country, a new understanding of God's
acts of salvation had already come to occupy the centre
of religious thought. The evangelical and Catholic revivals
had made people look at the biblical revelation in a fresh
light. In the theology of what is called the enlightenment,
which went side by side with the evidentialist apologetic,
the chief purpose of revelation was thought to have been
the communication of *truths* about God and human
destiny. Now it should not require a very profound knowledge of the Bible to realise that the communication of
information is only part of what revelation is all about.
The call and redemption of Israel in the Old Testament
and the life and power of the Kingdom brought by Christ
are Scripture's leading themes. The acts of God—including the apparently miraculous ones—therefore came
to the very centre of Christian thinking. Miracles had
previously been likened to seals on a document: but the
saving power of God as shown in the history of his people
was itself the good news and the proof of it.

This transformation of theology has no more striking illustration than the Church's teaching about our Lord's resurrection. In the theology of the enlightenment, it was looked upon as the crowning demonstration that the moral principles enunciated by Christ bore divine authority—it was, in a secondary way, a pledge of the future resurrection of believers. If we then turn to West-cott's *Gospel of the Resurrection*, 1865—a fine book which still repays study—we discover a very different point of view. For Westcott, the Resurrection is not an external attestation of the gospel, it *is* the gospel. Christ's manhood, victorious over sin, is taken triumphantly right through the experience of death, in order that it may be a per-petual seed of a new race of men. The works of power in Jesus' ministry also came to be viewed in a fresh way. The New Testament calls them *signs*; but of what? They were types of the spiritual miracles that Christ would work in the life of his Church.

The Bible does not lay the emphasis primarily upon the physical unusualness of the acts of God. It is concerned with certain combinations of events that are declared to be the revealing and saving work of God. Some of them do, of course, wear a physically transcendental appear-ance, but the Hebrews were not concerned with the way in which God brought them about. In one passage, the Red Sea is said to have been pushed back by a strong east wind. Everything that happened was caused in some way or other by God himself. The Hebrews did not know about Aristotle's distinction between primary and secon-dary causation, and if they had done, they would have thought it was irrelevant. Before we look further at the essence of miracle in the Bible, we must come to grips with our special modern perspective of the world.

The Rev. Dr. Ebenezer Cobham Brewer who gave us that delightful *Dictionary of Phrase and Fable* also compiled a *Dictionary of Miracles*, and here is an extract from it taken at random: "St. Regulus was exorcising a demon from a man. The demon said, 'If you cast me out, suffer me to enter the body of this ass.' And the bishop said 'Go'.When the devil was about to enter the ass, the beast (being apprised of his intention) made on the ground with his forefoot the sign of the cross; and the devil was obliged to pass on and leave the ass unmolested."

Nothing could better illustrate one of the greatest differences between the old world and our own. What makes the donkey story particularly useful as an illustration is that many of the topics discussed in books on science and religion simply do not touch it—whether natural causes played a part, whether the documents are reliable, and so on. We just don't believe this story. But why not? It is a sincere story with a religious moral. We do not believe that the universe we live in is the kind of place where things like this happen. This is not negative scepticism. Modern science arose in the heart of Christian Europe, where the orderliness of nature was believed to reflect the wisdom of God—it did not arise in the bosom of Buddhism; and it is ironical, incidentally, that some people should be looking to this faith as a refuge for twentieth-century man. It was no accident, moreover, that alongside the scientific discoveries of the Renaissance there came new visions in the arts and literature and the adventure of navigation that opened up the whole globe. What was being discovered was not only the Americas and the planets but new truths about man himself and his relation to his environment. Even the twentieth-century literature of despair is part of the same quest.

The adventure of modern medicine and the conquest of physical handicap has become a spiritual language which everyone understands. The story of Helen Keller means more to us than Brewer's whole dictionary of old-time miracles.

It is a great mistake to imagine, on the other hand, that man's so-called coming of age has altered his nature or total environment. The literature of other civilisations and centuries shows men worrying and grumbling about the same things as we do. Moreover, in the middle ages and the times of the Christian Fathers, when some men told stories like the one about the demon and the donkey, depths of spiritual insight were attained and written about which few of the readers of the *quality* newspapers today could comprehend.

All that has been said in this book about the coming of biblical theology fits into the modern scene. It is not a series of capitulations and weak compromises; it is part of the human voyage of discovery. It is, first, a hard journey back to the experience of the men of the Bible; and then, it is a quest into the unknown, taking *their* knowledge and faith with us into the strange world of the future. Modern historiography, which has often looked like a foe, has really been a great ally. For in the realm of secular history, students have been learning to do some of the very same things as biblical scholars do—to find out what men in past ages really believed and did.

In the Old Testament, we cannot now believe that God stopped the earth turning round one afternoon for the sake of Joshua's battle; the king who is supposed to have put Daniel in the lions' den never existed; but the real history has sprung to life. The real miracle is the people of God themselves, battered to pieces for nearly two millennia by predatory empires, yet with their faith intact, ever being renewed and purified.

The study of the New Testament has been dominated by the certainty that within the Christian records stands the genuinely human figure of Jesus. As we approach him he becomes more recognisably human, but he is not cut down to our size or made less mysterious—family and disciples could not fathom him, and even after the victory of Easter, his worshippers found it most helpful to stick to conceptual descriptions of him. We ought not to scale down our picture of manhood to contemporary evaluations—which in some respects are pathetic. The Bible says he is "a little lower than the angels"; whilst we seem content to be just a little higher than the brutes.

If we were more perceptive of the spiritual potentialities of manhood, we could see the ministry of Jesus, as the gospels do, as a conflict of power between the kingdom of God and the forces of evil; and even a conflict for the right use of power in the service of God. When we look at the deeds of Jesus, it is not possible to draw a line between what was achieved by a man whose mind and will were in perfect accord with God, and what could only have come about through the working of the transcendent Spirit through him. Scepticism about the power of mind over matter is as old-hat as the demon and the donkey. The real marvel of the gospel story, as Seeley saw, is not so much the presence of power but its control.

Jesus shows unbounded concern for people, and pours out his energy to loose the bonds that hold men's souls and bodies. To those who have eyes to see, these are the *signs of the kingdom*, he tells them. In the story of the temptations, we see him rejecting every false or misleading use of spiritual power. He refuses a miraculous sign to the

Pharisees, and tries to minimise the sensational effect of his work by enjoining silence upon those who were healed. The evangelists are loyal to him also by refraining from the use of some of the customary vocabulary of sensationalism. The fourth gospel pointedly uses the word *sign* for Jesus' works of power, and portrays Jesus making a sharp contrast between those who only came to gape and those who recognised what the signs meant.

This decisive attitude of Jesus is the very opposite of the wonder-worker: he is rejecting that caricature of religion in which God is made a substitute for personal self-giving—instead of what he really is, the fountain-head of our life. All that Jesus did and taught is driven home by the fact that he chose the way that led to the cross. This is both the supreme renunciation of power, and the focusing of power to achieve an infinitely fruitful victory.

The theological revolution by which we have come to be able to think of the Incarnation as a truly human experience ought to give us a vantage-point from which to see through the maze of our contemporary religious uncertainties. We are told that religion in its traditional form is irrelevant to the scientific age, because men have learned that the right thing to do is to attempt things for themselves, and not lean on supernatural aid. Danilo Dolci tells of a place in Sicily where priests and people went out day after day to chant a Latin litany for rain—when a 20 h.p. motor could have lifted enough water from the river to irrigate the whole parched district!

But the answer surely is, not that the Christian creed is wrong, but that men have persisted in trying to do exactly what the incarnate Lord refused to do. Jesus did not use the Godhead as a magical means of getting things done. He did not use the spiritual power of which he was conscious to override and coerce men. Day by day he poured out his life to the uttermost, in constant communion with the Father and the Spirit. The human body and mind was itself made to achieve the will of God and to reveal his glory and love. So we come back to the miracle of God's grace. By a divine metabolism, God makes it possible for man to pray and work and love, and so truly to live as a son in his Father's house.

INDEX